Relaxing in the hot springs!

CONTENTS

I Shall Survive Using Potions! Volume 4
by FUNA

Translated by Hiroya Watanabe
Edited by William Haggard
Layout by Leah Waig
English Cover & Lettering by Kelsey Denton

Copyright © 2019 FUNA
Illustrations by Sukima

First published in Japan in 2019 by Kodansha Ltd., Tokyo.
Publication rights for this English edition arranged through Kodansha Ltd., Tokyo.

Find more books like this one at www.j-novel.club!

President and Publisher: Samuel Pinansky
Managing Editor (Novels): Aimee Zink
QA Manager: Hannah N. Carter
Marketing Manager: Stephanie Hii

ISBN: 978-1-7183-7193-4
Printed in Korea
First Printing: March 2021
10 9 8 7 6 5 4 3 2 1

I SHALL SURVIVE USING POTIONS!

4

Author: FUNA
Illustrator: Sukima

Chapter 29:
Seaside Street

Here we are, at a coastal town!!

I decided to enjoy the seafood to the fullest before heading east toward the next country. I wasn't in any particular hurry, so I didn't really *have* to go anywhere, but after all that had happened, I felt like I should get moving sooner rather than later. I didn't want that crown prince guy to hear any rumors about me and decide to come over from the neighboring kingdom of Brancott, after all.

But if there was an entire other country between us, surely that would be too far for Fer-what's-his-face to come after me, right? Besides, I wanted to see what I could of this world before I found a companion to settle down with. It would be difficult to travel freely around the continent once I had a husband and children.

…That reminded me, what were Francette and Roland going to do?

Emile and Belle were orphans, and still quite young, so they could travel around for several years to train and gain experience before eventually settling down, or even go back to the kingdom of Balmore to live with the rest of the Eyes of the Goddess. Surely they would be skilled hunters by then, and could even open their own shop with the accumulated pay for their bodyguard services that I'd been stashing in the Item Box for them.

Well, I would leave that decision up to them. I was afraid they would say, "We want to live near you once you settle down and protect you for the rest of our lives!" but that, too, would be up to them. I had no right to complain, either way. No one can take responsibility for another person's life.

That left Fran and Roland. It wasn't like those two were lonely, rootless wanderers. They still had family in their home country, and Roland was royalty, for cryin' out loud! He couldn't just abandon his home, and if he ever had a kid, that child would inherit a claim to the throne unless the current king, Roland's younger brother, had his own child. Even if the king had children, there would still be the second and third claims to the throne, and so on...

They couldn't just wander around as they pleased indefinitely! Their home country, and whichever country they went to, wouldn't allow it.

Hmm, how long did these two plan on staying with me...? I didn't mind Emile and Belle, but it was like the other two were there to keep an eye on me, which was kind of hard to deal with...

Also, Fran and Roland had been in a bad mood the past few days, now that the lieutenant colonel had taken over their role as the "straight man" of the group.

...Not my problem!

"Let's find a place to stay first. Then we'll stuff our faces with all the seafood we can!" I declared to the others as we stood in front of the town, putting the chariot back into my Item Box.

I hadn't had a proper fish meal that wasn't dried or preserved in salt since being transported to this world. That was a bit rough for someone who had been born and raised in Japan. I did understand that there wasn't much that could be done for those who lived inland, considering the need to preserve and transport the fish, though.

I'd only been to a coastal town once before. But that was for an event when a new ship made by the Aligot Empire had arrived at the port of Balmore for the first time, and the purpose of the trip was to show me their completed vessel and thus earn my praise. So I was under siege by a bunch of shipwrights, and I had no time to walk around and enjoy the food, given all the parties and review meetings I had to attend.

And since it was a coastal town, I had assumed the fish would be cheap and their expensive cuisine would all be meat dishes, but they only had meat! Not only was there no seafood, they didn't even have vegetables! Why would there only be meat dishes in a coastal town?! What a load of crap!!!

Haah… Haah…

Well, at least there were no snobs around to claim that good meat had to be marbled, so I did enjoy the red meat at the restaurant, but I could have had that anywhere.

It's a coastal town, so just give me my fresh fish!

Well, in any case, that's how I missed my chance last time. But not this time! I was free to do what I wanted, so I was gonna eat all the seafood! Grilled and simmered fish were tempting, of course, but my mind was set on getting some sashimi. Sashimi was the only option! I'd eat it to my heart's content, then have grilled fish tomorrow, and simmered fish the day after.

And so, we entered the town and made our way toward the first fancy-looking restaurant I could find.

I wanted to eat as soon as possible, so I hurried the others along as they tied Ed up and we took our seats inside.

"Sashimi platters, please! I'll leave the selection to the chef!" I exclaimed to the waiter, without even looking at the menu on the table. The others were still reaching for their menus, but I didn't care! We didn't have to order everything at once anyway.

All right, it's time for sashimi! It's been years!!! I was totally pumped.

11

"…Sa-shi-mi?"

That is, until I got that response, complete with a perplexed expression…

"What is a sashimi?"

"…Huh?"

My language translation ability wasn't working? No, that couldn't be it!

"U-Um, it's raw fish that's cut into pieces and eaten…" I said, feeling shaken.

"Y-You want to eat raw fish?!" the waiter shouted in surprise, which turned all eyes in the restaurant toward us.

What? They didn't eat sashimi? Well, it's true that the royal capital and every other location I'd visited only served fish dried or preserved in salt, but I thought that was just out of necessity, for preservation and transportation to the inland cities, and so forth.

I had assumed that a coastal town would offer raw fish, or at least similar dishes, like tataki, carpaccio, or namero. I mean, I thought fishermen everywhere had cut and trimmed freshly caught fish, scooped out the innards with their fingers, then rinsed the fish with seawater and eaten them, basically since forever…

So why was I getting looks like I had just said something utterly inconceivable…?

"Hey, buddy, you should explain properly. Anyone who eats a fish that hasn't been fully cooked will get bugs in their stomach and end up rolling around in pain. I mean, I guess inlanders who don't eat raw fish wouldn't know this, but if you try to cook one without knowing how, your whole group'll end up needing a visit to a doctor." One of the tough-looking customers thus offered a friendly warning. He kinda looked like a ruffian, but was smiling as he spoke. Maybe he was a fisherman?

"...Ah, you're talking about parasites!"

"Oh, you know about 'em?" the older dude, I mean, *gentleman*, said with a surprised look.

...I'd been kind of sloppy with my word choice since coming to this world, so I had to be careful. My brother always used to say, "Your eyes are pretty scary, so you'd have no redeeming qualities if you had a dirty mouth, too..." Hey, shut it!

In Japan, they say you shouldn't eat river fish raw, but sea fish are fine, though that's just because it's commonly known that most saltwater fish were treated by freezing them before being distributed. Most freshwater fish weren't treated this way. Moreover, sea fish lived far away from humanity, so their parasites didn't evolve to target humans as a host.

In other words, most parasites for saltwater fish that enter a human body don't last long, and could only ever manage to cause temporary pain, albeit rather excruciating pain, without generating any potentially lethal symptoms.

...Well, a couple hours of excruciating pain was bad enough already.

Conversely, rivers and swamps are a part of the land on which humans live.

They live alongside land animals, so a lot of parasites in freshwater fish could survive in the bodies of those animals.

What I'm trying to say is, some of them were really dangerous to eat. That's probably why eating raw freshwater fish was known to be a bad idea.

Anyway, it wasn't that sea fish didn't have any parasites. If they hadn't been frozen and checked by the fish shop to remove them manually, they were actually pretty common, like the kind that causes extreme pain in the human body. I knew all of this, but

I could easily deal with toxins and parasites with my potions, so I didn't really worry about them.

...But, of course, a restaurant would. Even if I told them that I didn't mind the risks, there was no way they could serve raw fish. If someone got sick at their establishment, it would negatively impact their reputation.

"Grilled and simmered fish, one dish each, chef's choice..." Feeling defeated, I ordered without looking at the menu or giving it much thought.

One by one, Francette and the others ordered as well. It seemed they actually perused the menu first.

Francette went on and on as she placed her order. Yeah, her body required a lot of food to fuel her physical abilities.

That's why she ate a ton, but... she never got fat. Ugh!

As such, I was still in a state of total hopelessness as the food arrived. It all tasted good! Damn it!

"Would you mind letting me borrow your kitchen?" I asked the owner of our inn, after we booked a room and took a little break. If I couldn't get sashimi at a restaurant, I would just have to make my own. I was already used to making sashimi in my previous world, after all.

Growing up in a family of five, it was better to buy fish in blocks rather than getting the pre-cut kind. That is, the blocks weren't necessarily cheaper, but freshly sliced fish tasted better than fish that was cut earlier that morning. The cross-section of store-bought sashimi is exposed to air for a long time, so the flavor definitely degrades over time. I'd much rather take a well-sharpened sashimi kitchen knife and slice the fish with one smooth, swift motion, so as to not squish the meat as I cut it, then add a pinch of freshly grated wasabi and... Ohhh!

"Oh, what kind of dish do you want to make? We're prepping right now, so we're not serving customers yet. I don't mind you using it for a bit, but I'd have to watch to make sure you don't do anything dangerous or damage the equipment."

Yes!

My decision to choose a cheap inn because it was likely to be more easygoing had paid off.

"Sashimi. Umm, it's a dish where you cut raw fish into thin strips, then eat it with condiments! I have my own condiments, so if you could just let me borrow a kitchen knife and cutting board…"

"I can't let you do that."

Huh? He'd just said I could! I glared at him reflexively, and he visibly cringed, with a tight expression on his face.

"Th-Threatening me won't do you any good! O-Of course I can't let you!"

I wasn't threatening him, and he didn't have to be so scared… Well, never mind. I already knew.

"Why?!"

The owner's look changed to one of exasperation as he replied.

"We're an inn and eatery. If word gets out that a guest had writhed around in pain and was sent to the doctor after eating here, we'd go out of business!"

"Ah…"

He had a point. The part about the guest making the food herself would be the first detail to get omitted as the rumors spread. Then they would be ridiculously exaggerated and embellished, turning them into malicious rumors that people spread for fun. Not unlike the environment of the internet on Earth…

"What if I promise you I'll be fine…?"

"The answer's still no. I have way too much to lose by taking a risk and trusting the words of a child I just met."

"Thought so!"

He was right. I would absolutely say the same thing in his place. And so I gave up and went back to my room.

For dinner, I ate the grilled and simmered fish I had gotten from the restaurant. I just couldn't be bothered, knowing I couldn't have sashimi…

Feeling heartbroken, I went to bed with Layette early. Yes, to prepare for the coming morning.

*   *

"I'm going out for a walk."

I tried to carry Layette in my arms and… whoa, she's heavy!

Early in the morning, I had embarked on a grief-stricken journey, holding Layette's hand. No one had tried to speak to me, likely out of consideration for my state of despair. And while nobody followed me out, I knew they were going to stay out of sight and watch over me.

Enshrouded in sorrow, there was only one place for me to go.

Yes, the market. The fish market! If I couldn't borrow a kitchen, I would just have to prepare everything myself. I'd get my own ingredients and kitchen!

And here we are, at the fish market!

Of course, it wasn't just merchants from neighboring towns and villages that were there to stock up on goods. The general population could buy things, too. They weren't auctioning anything off, or selling exclusively in the early morning, or anything like that.

It was more like a gathering of retailers selling their wares out of street stalls, so it was no problem for an outsider like me to be there.

Each shop seemed to have merchants, or the wives and daughters of fishermen, tending it. They were calling out boisterously to customers... I wondered how they didn't ruin their throats, yelling like that all day. Maybe a woman with a hoarse voice was a sign of a hard-working wife?

Then there were silent saleswomen... Oh, maybe they were going for guys who weren't fishermen? Guess there were all sorts of ways to go about it.

I wasn't particularly good at telling quality fish apart, but I could probably just buy whatever and be okay. Everything there should have just been caught by the fishermen of this town, so they should all be alike in terms of freshness.

It was also unlikely that someone would sell something poisonous to a young girl without any warning... I mean, it was possible they really were selling poisonous fish. Even on Earth, there were people who liked the tingling sensation that came from the poison in fugu.

Looking around, there were all sorts of fish I knew…or, rather, fish that resembled the kinds I knew, and some I'd never seen before. Just because I'd never seen them before, though, didn't mean they didn't exist on Earth.

Fish I'd seen and recognized from fish shops, supermarkets, aquariums, books, and TV were only a tiny fraction of those that existed on Earth.

The minor ones that didn't have much market value were probably eaten by the fishermen and their families, without ever hitting the market. Those were known as fisherman's fish. They may not have much monetary value, but it wasn't that they tasted bad. It was simply that they weren't worth much, mainly because of their appearance, or due to being unknown.

In places like Okinawa, you could find blue fish being sold normally. And by blue fish, I don't mean mackerel, pacific saury, or sardines. Those weren't fully blue, they just had some blue on their spines.

But in Okinawa, there were fish that were actually blue… like the knobsnout parrotfish.

So, what I'm saying is, even if I don't recognize a fish, it may just be that I don't know anything about it, and they could be sold and eaten normally in other countries or fishing villages somewhere on Earth.

But for today, I wasn't going to challenge any unknowns. I'd go for fish that were as close to the ones I knew as possible.

Hmm, I doubt they did any deep-sea fishing, so there probably wouldn't be any tuna or whale meat. Though, I guess it would be possible to get that inland, instead. They just wouldn't be guaranteed to be in stock every day. That is, assuming there were tuna and whales in this world, and they happened to live in this region.

And so, I picked some seafood without putting too much thought into it, and put it all into the big bag I had brought with me. I had stuffed the bag with filling beforehand, so I could pretend to put it into the bag while actually putting anything I got into the Item Box, instead.

There was nobody watching me while I went shopping (besides a certain female knight and her companions) so no one would realize I was putting more seafood into the bag than it could physically contain. So, I got an inada-looking one, a hamachi-looking one, and a buri-looking one... Wait, those were all the same fish!

Oh, I guess their names don't change based on their sizes here. No promotions for them, I guess.

I bought a bunch of shellfish and seaweed, too. They could be used to make miso soup, and I liked the texture of whelk.

Ah, they're selling gooseneck barnacles. I didn't know they existed in this world... Strange creatures, those things. They were actually crustaceans, but a type that clung to rock walls and just stayed there. I had heard they're distant cousins of the acorn barnacle. They looked like turtle hands, and were actually pretty tasty. Peeling the outer skin is kind of a hassle, though.

I decided to buy some.

"Those are creepy..."

Layette had been looking around sparkly-eyed at the unique atmosphere and the array of seafood, but chimed in with a complaint. I mean, they did look like chopped-off turtle hands... though I wasn't sure if Layette had ever actually seen a turtle before.

My shopping continued along smoothly. No weirdos tried to mess with me, either.

Fishing villages and towns with a prominent fishing industry tended to have a lot of tough guys and a well-established hierarchy of influential people, like fisherman bosses, leaving little room for gangs or thugs to butt in. These men worked every day putting their lives on the line, and there was no way they'd stay quiet if someone messed with their families and friends. Nor would the fisherman bosses, after having their revenue source...I mean, precious employees...meddled with. In other words, there were no child kidnappers or sections of town overtaken by rowdy street punks.

Yeah, it was a nice place.

Once I had finished buying a bunch of fresh seafood, I went back to the inn in a pretty good mood. I would eat normal, cooked seafood at the inn and dining hall for today, and go sightseeing in town. I also wanted to check how advanced the ocean-related technology was here. Like how good their naval engineering and navigation were, for example.

Well, I was planning on going down the seaside road, so I didn't have to look into everything in this town, specifically. I could look around for a little bit, then research some more in a different, bigger city. This was just a small, rural village, after all.

All right, I'm gonna leave this town tomorrow and make some sashimi where no one will bother me!

*   *

It was just before noon, the following day. I forget what happened after buying seafood at the market. It wasn't important. I looked around, ate, then went to sleep. That was all.

I woke up early this morning, then left without eating breakfast. Then I made my way along the road on the seaside, and it was finally lunchtime.

"All right, it's time for lunch!"

"…Kaoru, isn't it a bit early for lunch?" Francette objected, but I ignored her.

Unlike me, who intended to put everything on the line for this meal, everyone else had already eaten breakfast. But I didn't care! I couldn't wait a second longer!

"It's already past 9AM."

Everyone else yelled, "That's way too early!!!"

Doesn't matter!

I picked a spot to leave the road and descend toward the coast. I settled on a spot that had a nice view and couldn't be seen from the road, with plenty of tree cover, then took out a tent for shade, along with a table and chairs, then told the others to rest there.

As for me…

"Worktable, cutting board, knife, tableware, imitation wasabi, imitation soy sauce, water tank…"

One after another, I pulled out the necessary things from the Item Box and laid them out on the table. The water tank, which I had created before as a potion container, came with a stand and a valve near the bottom. It could be used as a water supply in a pinch. It looked like a wooden barrel at first glance, but it was actually made with reinforced plastic.

Then, it was time to bring it out. Yes, the raw fish I had obtained yesterday!

"Come forth, ingredients!"

And so, not the Kitchen Stadium, but rather the Kitchen Colosseum, had appeared.

"Allez cuisine!"

I quickly prepped the fish. I took off the scales, removed the head, extracted the spine, cut out the abdominal segment, then picked off the bones that were left on it. The whole segment left together would be too big to use, so I cut it into a block that would be easier to slice into sashimi.

Now I could turn it into sashimi, sear and marinate it into a tataki, or cook it anyway I wanted.

I put the block back into the Item Box to prevent the flavor from degrading. Then, it was on to the other dishes.

Unlike me, the others probably wouldn't be satisfied with just sashimi. The horse-mackerel-looking fish would be salt-grilled. I'd simmer some of the amberjack-looking one and teriyaki the rest. I'd had a lot of simmered and grilled fish in the past two days, but I was going to use Japanese seasonings and condiments, like the imitation soy sauce, and feed them to the others.

Once I finished getting the other dishes ready, I took the fish block I had prepped for sashimi out of the Item Box again. Now, to deal with the problem.

Antidote/healing potion, inside a container shaped like a bracelet, that can be controlled with my brain waves, to dissolve and eliminate parasites, bacteria, and other toxic substances, come out!

Then, a bracelet appeared on my right wrist just like I had imagined. I was afraid it could get lost or stolen if I could take it off, so I made it unremovable.

…What if I wanted to take it off? I could just put it back in the Item Box. If I wanted to put it back on, I could make it appear on my wrist again.

What's that? A bandit could cut off my hand and take it? No, no. No bandit would injure prey that could be sold on the black market as a slave at a high price. The bracelet didn't look like it was made of expensive metal, and there weren't any jewels on it, either.

If someone questioned why I wouldn't take it off, I'd tell them that it was family tradition to leave it on, and I had done so since I was young.

This bracelet would warn me with a tingling sensation when there were parasites, bacteria, or toxic substances nearby. And if I mentally willed it, those substances would be dissolved. It would be soundless and undetectable by anyone watching, of course.

The reason I didn't make it trigger automatically was because that would break down all medicine with even a hint of toxicity, so all sorts of chemical substances would be toast. As soon as I stepped into a drugstore, their entire stock would be wiped out. This could affect merchants and their carts full of wares as I passed by, too.

And if someone tried to poison me and was caught, the evidence would be completely destroyed. That's why I made it so it would just warn me, and the actual elimination would be done at my will.

The effective range could be adjusted too. I kept it at a 30cm radius by default, so I could detect anything on a plate in front of me, or food at the end of my chopsticks or my fork. And if I wanted to include my friends in my effective range, I'd adjust it as needed.

Bzzz…

Ohh, it had detected something already…

Many types of parasites reside in the skin or the internal organs, but some of them move into the muscles once their host has died. I'd removed the outer skin and organs, but maybe they had already migrated into the meat, or it was a type of parasite that infested the meat section to begin with…

Actually, it could've been some sort of pathogen, accumulated heavy metals, or toxins contained in some creature the fish had eaten, and not necessarily a parasite. Taking all that into consideration…

Eliminate!

The area of effect would, of course, include everything on and around the table. I wasn't sure if eliminating them dissolved them at a subatomic level or sent them away somewhere...

Even if they were rendered dead and harmless, I didn't want to eat a parasite, so I'd be fine with it regardless, as long as I knew there were no parasite corpses in my food.

So, I'd leave the method up to the "Goddess Workshop." I had no problem with how it worked as long as she chose a method that was easy and convenient.

Oh, I should take out all the seafood from the Item Box later, purify it, and then store it again. I just felt like getting it all done at once, since I didn't want to do this process every single time.

And it was done! Kaoru's special full-course seafood! Even though there was sashimi, no one here would refuse to eat it out of an abundance of caution. This was a meal cooked by a goddess's own hands, after all.

Not to mention, I had made them because *I* wanted to eat them. It was highly unlikely to be dangerous, and no one would doubt a goddess who they trusted unconditionally and in whom they placed their faith.

...Besides Roland, that is.

Emile, Belle, Francette, and Layette immediately began munching away at the sashimi. Roland was the only one who avoided it.

There were small bottles of wasabi and soy sauce for the sashimi.

"Delicious!"

"Mmm, this is so good!"

They didn't just like the simmered and grilled dishes, but the sashimi was also a hit! It actually tasted even better after being aged a bit. The texture was better when fresh, but aging it would bring out the umami far more. But if you messed up the preparation or aged it for too long, it would decay. It required far too much knowledge for an amateur to try. I didn't care about all that for now, though.

All right, time to eat!

*   *

We headed southeast, along the seaside road.

The peninsula jutting out of the west side of the continent ended and turned into a part of the main body, so the perimeter was expanding to the south.

The occasional fishing villages we saw only had a few small boats, if any.

I'd heard that this country was working on constructing ocean-going ships to expand into the islands to the west of the Kingdom of Aligot, but that was probably happening in the bigger port towns or even the naval ports.

…Well, supposedly, bigger port towns and naval ports hadn't even existed until recently. They only existed on a much smaller scale. Like, just ports at small fisherman villages.

But now, countries along the sea were in the middle of a shipbuilding renaissance. They were working on serious ocean-going ships modeled after the historical carracks from Earth, with a focus on transportation capacity.

Of course, these were made with the knowledge I had brought over as a base, and I had given Aligot the edge at first, but since then I'd given each country equal treatment and they all had the same documents. It was still too early to reveal the compact and mobile caravels and the improved form of carracks known as galleons.

Incidentally, the *Santa Maria* that Columbus sailed to the New World and the *Victoria*, the ship Magellan and his crew used to sail around the world, were also carracks.

It was a bit surprising to see how small they are by modern Japanese standards. Caravels were basically from the same era. They're a bit small, but boast superior mobility and speed. Caravels served as the consort ships of Columbus's *Santa Maria*, and the two ships used by Columbus and his crew to return home were the very same model.

Galleons were what later became the basis for the ship of the line, and I was afraid those would lead to an outbreak of naval warfare, so I was a bit hesitant to spread this knowledge. The high carrying capacity of the carrack, and the swiftness and maneuverability of the caravel, should've been more than enough.

They could improve upon the technology without any further help from Earth knowledge from this point on.

I'd be fraught with guilt if they ended up progressing in a strange direction and the standard ended up being catamaran battleships or ships that could combine multiple units into one like the Apollo Norm.

Chapter 30:
Meanwhile...

"What?!"

Fernand rose from his seat reflexively upon hearing the report from his subordinate.

"Kaoru is in the Kingdom of Jusral right now?"

The report stated that the messenger and the Goddess Celestine had appeared in the neighboring Kingdom of Jusral and had saved it from imminent danger. Not only that, but the messenger had been running a medicine shop in the royal capital of Jusral for some time.

"It's Kaoru! I don't know whether it's alpha or beta, but that doesn't matter. In any case, we must find her and bring her back here. Prepare to leave immediately!"

Fernand, the crown prince of the Kingdom of Brancott, was certain that "Alfa Kaoru Nagase" was the same Kaoru who had been working as a waitress at that restaurant.

There couldn't be two women like her...

Indeed, there were the battles in the Aligot Empire, at the peace conference, and the many episodes over the course of the four years after. Those were more than enough confirmation.

Her stopping by the restaurant she used to work at as she passed through Brancott couldn't be a coincidence, either.

I'll bring her back, no matter what... Fernand resolved to himself, but Fabio had a disapproving look on his face as he watched Fernand.

If Kaoru had been a citizen of his country... And if she had been an ordinary person... If that was the case, Fernand could have applied pressure to get what he wanted, being the crown prince of a powerful kingdom.

But being from another country and having been given superhuman powers by the Goddess Celestine, as well as permission to use them as she pleased if she happened across injustice, Kaoru wasn't someone who would be cowed by demands simply because they came from the son of the ruler of a kingdom of men.

...This wasn't going to end well. But no amount of reasoning would convince Fernand to give up. Fabio had known him long enough to understand this.

Besides, the chances of it working weren't necessarily zero. Even if they were one in a thousand, or one in ten thousand, they were still greater than zero...

*　　　*

After stuffing my face with seafood at the seaside, I proceeded down the main road for a few days, eventually ending up at a medium-sized city. The city faced the sea, and even though it had a small port, it wasn't exactly booming with maritime trade. Ships, the sea trade, and large-scale fishing still hadn't developed enough in this world. The Aligot Empire was the only nation that had proper blue-water sailing vessels up to this point.

But many of these ships were currently in construction in various countries, and once finished, maritime trade would likely prosper, leading to the rapid development of existing and new port towns. Moreover, it was said that a new type of ship was being constructed in this town with the combined effort of the entire country behind it.

I was thinking I wanted to get a look at it when the ship entered port. It was small by my standards, but everyone here would consider it to be a properly massive ship. Also, the sailing ship was equipped with a strangely familiar figurehead with scary-looking eyes at its bow...

Yes, it was certainly the Aligot Empire's new-model sailing ship. It wasn't all that impressive yet, but it was capable of crossing the ocean while loaded up with crew and goods, putting it a step above the boats that had been used up until now.

Yes, I helped raise that thing! No, really. I contributed in various ways, like providing model ships I created as potion containers and suggestions on improving their shipboard compasses.

...When they started asking about the firing holes for the cannons, though, I somehow managed to avoid mentioning their real purpose. Right now, they're being used as windows for letting in light and fresh air. Someone may eventually realize their true purpose and use them as firing holes for arrows, spears, and ballistas, but that's on them, and certainly none of my concern.

I'd seen the inside of a ship from the Aligot Empire in the past, when I stopped by the Kingdom of Balmore's northern port. It was pretty much the same model, so I didn't much care to look at this one. More importantly, I didn't want them to notice me and start making a fuss.

So, even though I wanted to check out the current construction of this world's first large-scale sailing ship, I decided not to bother visiting the imperial shipyard.

...But then I found out that not only had the ships of this country not been rigged yet, but that it would be some time before even the hull was finished being built.

Though, thinking about it, I guess it wasn't really that surprising. Even when some higher-ups suddenly order you to start

31

working on such a project, you can lose months on problems with the budget, rights and interests, facilities, engineers, and plenty of other obstacles.

Even the Kingdom of Balmore and the Kingdom of Aseed had just recently finished small prototype ships and were still working on their large-scale models, so it made sense that other countries still had a ways to go.

The Aligot Empire was the truly abnormal one, what with having large-scale sailing ships already in service. Well, I suppose other countries could hardly compete when, to the Aligot Empire, failure isn't an option, and they'd consequently poured all of their resources into the project.

All right, I'm skipping this city and moving on to the next.

"Lady Kaoru!"

Gyaaaaaa!

"Y-You must have the wrong person…"

"No, there's no mistaking those eyes!"

Shut up!

Looking more carefully, I realized that I recognized this person. He was one of the Aligot Empire's engineers. I remembered the discussions we'd had before.

Using only model ships as references, I remembered having heated debates about how to use square sails and fore-and-aft sails, about dynamic lift and drag, about how to maintain the shape of the expanded sail, and about how to suppress the loss of air current against the sails. I was an amateur, and one who only had knowledge gleaned from movies, novels, and manga, while they were engineers who lacked firsthand knowledge but made up for it with abnormal sharpness, and we had spent our days testing our theories with small boats.

...Those were fun times.

Even though I'm a normie and an amateur, I felt like I had become a cutting-edge engineer at the forefront of scientific development. I got to experience what it was like to be one of the top-class technicians of this world.

Having top-secret meetings and conducting experiments with the Aligot Empire's design group, while trying not to get caught by the Kingdom of Balmore's own engineers, had been incredibly thrilling.

I had so much fun...

As I stood, reminiscing, the engineer seemed to have lost his patience and opted to make a bold move.

"If you insist on denying it, you leave me no choice!"

With that, he drew in a deep breath, and...

"Ah! It's the great friend of the Goddess, Kao—"

"Stop that!" I quieted him with a swift punch to the gut.

He crumpled in pain, clutching his stomach, but that wasn't my problem. He deserved it!

"Th-That was cruel..." he said, with a reproachful tone, after finally recovering from the blow. He had basically blackmailed me, so I didn't apologize.

"That's what you get for trying to make such a disturbance when I'm keeping a low profile!"

"I'm sorry..."

The people of the Aligot Empire should really have known by now that it's not a good idea to make me upset. Even if he was desperate to keep me from escaping, he also seemed to realize he had made a mistake, and was very apologetic about the whole situation.

I supposed I could forgive him...

"So, what is it you want from me?"

"Oh, no, I don't need anything in particular. Of course I'd want to talk to you when I happen to see you at a place like this! I would love for you to see this ship, because we're incredibly proud of it, and if you could possibly offer some opinions and advice…"

I could hardly blame him for thinking that way. I guess that wasn't too much to ask…

And so, I took the others with me to board the ship. Yup, without cannons on board, it was more like an army ship than a naval battleship. For naval combat, they must have used marine soldiers, and if it came down to it, the members of the crew could have picked up swords and fought.

I figured the main purpose of this ship was the transportation of goods and men, anyway, not combat. It may have been military men operating the ship, but maybe it was more appropriate to call it a transport.

After taking a closer look, I thought they had accomplished a lot in such a short time, what with using only a model ship as a reference and having none of the basic technology beforehand. A professional must have done the strength calculations and such, but there were fewer leaks than I expected, and the sails had been upgraded from the time I had been there to help plan out the design.

Yeah, they were doing a good job. I was the one who had raised these 'kids,' after all!

"Kaoru… This figurehead…"

Okay, let's get out of here!

What are you all doing? It's time to go! On to the next city!

Damn it!

*   *

"What? She's already gone?"

Fernand, Crown Prince of Brancott, had finally arrived at the neighboring Kingdom of Jusral's capital, Litenia, only to find that all that was left of Layette's Atelier was an empty storefront. Caught by surprise, he had his attendants search the surrounding shops, but they all said the same thing: the Angel had departed to fulfill her next mission.

Fernand's group had gone straight to Layette's Atelier, despite having claimed that this was a courtesy visit to the king, and he finally decided to head over to the royal palace. This was, of course, to gather information about Kaoru.

"What? She left the country already?"

He even asked about Kaoru during his audience with the king.

This was considered extremely rude, of course, but the king quickly surmised what this was all about from the way Fernand acted and therefore responded with a forced smile. Fabio and Alan, who had accompanied Fernand, bowed their heads apologetically behind their crown prince.

They felt quite anxious about the whole thing, given that it had the potential to devolve into a major diplomatic *faux pas*. Fortunately for them, the king was a gracious man.

Fernand was no fool. Normally, there was no way he would act in such a manner. He was generally able to handle most diplomacy flawlessly, so Fabio hadn't been worried about this meeting with the king, and thus the error had come entirely unexpectedly. It seemed that all of his reasoning abilities flew out the window when it came to Kaoru.

Alan pinched Fernand's butt from behind, shocking him back to his senses. Fernand finally paid his respects with all proper courtesy, but still asked about Kaoru again later on.

"I see. So, wishing to avoid a commotion, she has headed east without returning to the royal capital..."

"Indeed. To think, she may have decided to stay here if that had not happened... It truly is a shame. But it would have been truly arrogant to ask for such a thing after she saved our kingdom from danger. Upon saving us, the Angel has departed to fulfill her next task. All we could do was give her our full appreciation..."

"..."

The king wanted to tell the young and inexperienced prince that he should not be so attached to the Angel, and that even though Fernand was royalty, there were some things he must not try to make his own. However, the message didn't seem to get through to the crown prince, and the king could only force himself to smile again.

Fabio and Allan had picked up on the message, of course, but remained exasperated by Fernand, who suddenly turned into an idiot when it came to matters involving Kaoru.

When the group had expressed their gratitude and was preparing to leave, the king called out to Fernand.

"When you return, would you be so kind as to pass along a message to your father?"

"Yes, of course. What would you like to tell him?"

The king replied, "Good. 'If you wish for me to forget about your son's many discourtesies, hand over half of that secret wine collection you were boasting about a while back.' Please tell him I said that."

"Huh...?"

37

At that moment, Fernand finally came to understand how remiss he had been with his lack of etiquette during this visit, and that his attitude had completely given away that he had only come to gather information on Kaoru.

"M-My apologies! I-I've displayed such insolent behavior... I do beg your forgiveness..." Fernand desperately bowed his head, but the king waved his hand with a laugh.

"It's no matter... Well, I suppose I shouldn't say that. Listen closely. If I had been any other ruler, this could have been a major incident, or you may have been subject to punitive demands in response. Although, knowing him, having half of his beloved wine collection taken from him may be more than enough punishment.

"In any case, you must be more conscious of your position and of the responsibilities you carry on your shoulders. Otherwise, you may lose something far more important than your father's wine. Be it your honor, the lives of your people, or something else entirely... Take this to heart, crown prince of the Kingdom of Brancott! And do not forget to pass along my message about the wine!"

...That would've been a nice speech if he had left that last part out.

And so, Fernand checked into a room at the finest inn in the capital. He had, of course, made a reservation before coming out here. This was merely a courtesy visit, and he hadn't come as an official guest, so he couldn't stay overnight at the royal palace.

"What will you do, Fernand?"

"...I have no choice. Even if I headed east now, Kaoru will already be gone. If I had laid the proper groundwork in my visit here, I may have gotten away with saying 'I happened to meet up with an old friend, we hit it off, and so we went back home together,' but if

I go to yet another country without any warning, act suspiciously, then take a girl from a foreign land back with me, I'd have serious trouble when the national authorities found out..."

"Ah, it seems you still have some capacity to think rationally. I'm relieved."

"Now listen here..."

Fernand looked displeased at Fabio's expression of relief. But with the near-incident he had been responsible for at the palace earlier, he couldn't get too upset.

"Then shall we return home?" asked Fabio.

Of course, Fernand hadn't come with just himself and his two friends. It was an official courtesy visit by the crown prince to a neighboring realm, so they had a decent-sized party with them, one that included attendants and guards.

They had to return as soon as they were done with their business, or they would create endless trouble for the attendants and other staff who were performing their regular duties without the rest of their colleagues. He had brought them this far for his own benefit, despite the trouble it had caused. He couldn't continue to be selfish like this.

"I suppose I have no choice..." Fernand said, then a voice spoke to him from his side.

"...I'll go."

"Huh?" Fernand and Fabio blurted in unison.

"Allan? What are you..."

"It'd be problematic for you to go around without making prior arrangements first, Fernand. Besides, all these attendants and guards make you incredibly conspicuous, and sneaking around with just the three of us sounds fun, but it just wouldn't fly. If you had been a third son or something, maybe, but you're the crown prince..."

Fernand stayed silent, a sour expression on his face.

"So, I have an idea. I, holder of the title 'least noble-looking guy in the world,' who is often said to look like a simple huntsman or guard behind my back, will go after her by myself. Once you get home, I want you to write an official letter assigning me the task of pursuing the Angel, and hand it to my father. That way, I can act freely, since I'm on an official mission from the crown prince. And since I'm just the son of an ordinary noble, it won't be an issue if I go to other countries without prior notice. What do you think? Good idea, right?"

"Allan, you…"

"…You just want to do this because it sounds like a fun adventure, don't you?!" Fernand and Fabio shouted in unison.

Fabio followed up with another accusation.

"And you wouldn't even come back if you do manage to find Kaoru! You're plotting to stick with her and follow her on her travels while leaving me to take care of Fernand!"

A bead of sweat rolled down Allan's head as he averted his eyes.

Then Fernand turned to Fabio, shouting, "What do you mean 'take care of' me?!"

Their room was rather noisy, despite it being late at night, but no one dared complain…

*   *

When Fernand awakened the next morning, Allan was nowhere to be seen. Instead, he found a single letter…

"Send that letter to my father for me. I'll handle the rest!"

"He got us!!!" the two remaining men yelled.

Allan had snuck out of the inn late in the night, taken his horse out of the stable, and ridden off onto the main road with glee. He was headed, of course, east from the capital.

There had been only starlight illuminating his path when he had left, but he was under no particular time constraint, so it was safe for him to travel as long as he went slowly. Fernand's group wouldn't pursue him, anyway, and he only had to make enough distance so they'd think he had gotten away completely, and therefore he decided to walk his horse at a leisurely pace until daybreak.

He would pass through the village Kaoru had saved, continue east, then head to the neighboring country. Judging by Kaoru's movements up to this point, it was clear that she was staying in each region as long as she felt like doing so, rather than rushing off to a certain destination.

This meant that Allan had no reason to rush, either. His task was quite simple: he just needed to look around the local inns, medicine shops, and boxed lunch shops for any unusual rumors whenever he stopped in a mid-sized city.

Kaoru left traces at every stop, almost as if she had no intention of hiding her whereabouts. Maybe she really didn't. She was just traveling around and helping people, seemingly at random, and it wasn't as if she was running away from anyone. Allan had a feeling this was an opportunity to say goodbye to a boring life. This thought put him in a good mood.

Allan continued along his path, humming as he did so. He passed through the village to the east, then continued moving eastward until the intersection with the road stretching to the north and south, then...

Chapter 31: Beliscas

The group crossed over the border, out of the Kingdom of Jusral, and entered the eastern land of Beliscas.

This country did have a king, but it didn't operate under an absolute monarchical system. It was actually more like a republic, though it wasn't fully considered one, nor was it a complete democracy either.

That was why it didn't have a particular appellation, and was simply referred to as Beliscas. Its capital, Jammus, was located roughly in the center of the country.

"What should we do, Kaoru? We already crossed the border, but if you want to go to the capital city, we'll need to head northeast..."

"Oh, we'll keep going along the ocean for now..." Kaoru said, cutting off Francette's comment. It had been a while since Kaoru had seen the ocean, so she wanted to maintain that view for a little while longer.

Since marine transportation and the fishing industry still hadn't flourished on this continent, there weren't many countries with their capitals on the land near the coast, so you needed to go inland to get to the royal and imperial capitals. And now that they were on the main section of the continent, rather than on the peninsulas, there was a lot of internal territory that didn't face the sea. Therefore, they would've had to leave the coastline eventually, anyway.

Although, they didn't necessarily have to move inland, unless there was some specific reason to go to the capital... Regardless, Kaoru and her party continued down the coastal road.

"Oh, there's a city up ahead," Emile called out from the head of the group, and sure enough, a cluster of buildings could be seen in the distance.

They could see a substantial distance from the bend in the road they were walking on, and thus could tell that it would still be some time before they arrived at the town. They were in no particular hurry, of course, and continued moving at a leisurely pace.

"It seems to be a fairly big place. What do you think, Kaoru?"

"Hmm, we already crossed the border, so maybe we'll stay there. I wouldn't mind living there for a while, if it's a nice place." Kaoru replied to Francette.

Roland frowned slightly, since it would be unfortunate if she actually decided to take up permanent residence elsewhere.

Emile and Belle actually wanted Kaoru to return to Balmore and live with the other orphans in the Eyes of the Goddess, but they had no intention of pushing their own desires onto her, or trying to influence her decisions.

As for Francette, Kaoru was her main priority. She wanted to follow Kaoru wherever she went, but knew she likely couldn't keep that up with Roland tagging along, given that he was royalty.

If only I had come alone.

If only Roland wasn't here.

Francette couldn't stop those thoughts from lingering in her mind.

Maybe I got married too quickly...

No, we aren't married quite yet.

I could still call off the marriage…

Roland would likely fall unconscious if he ever found out those thoughts were in her head.

Kaoru had given Francette a chance at marriage after she had given up, and now Francette was considering abandoning her future partner to stay by Kaoru's side. She was completely at a loss as to what her priorities were.

"Kaoru, I wanted to ask you for a favor…" Francette approached Kaoru to make a direct appeal.

"What is it?"

"I want to be someone who can live with you in your next 'backstory.' It's a bit too difficult to keep watch over you at all times when we live in separate residences…"

"Of course it would be difficult! What did… Wait, why were you watching me at all times in the first place?!" Kaoru yelled with exasperation, but didn't notice Francette hadn't used the phrase 'we' or 'us' in her proposal.

But Roland, who had noticed this little detail, turned pale at the realization.

*   *

We finally arrived at the entrance of the city. It had taken some time to get here after we had first spotted the buildings in the distance.

Hmm, what sort of job would let me have interactions with the locals…

The medicine shop idea ended up being a failure. I mean, it made a decent profit, but it failed to assist with my main objective of having a quiet life, blending in with the residents of the city, and finding a good husband. The boxed lunch business had been a hit, but the prep needed to mass-produce them every day was a bit too much work.

This time, I wanted to take it easy.

But then again, most jobs *weren't* easy, and I wouldn't have opportunities to meet guys outside of the workplace if I worked every day.

Since I didn't have skills that translated into anything that might get me hired as a professional in this world, my only options for working normally, without standing out by using my cheat abilities, were things like clerking, factory jobs, and other straightforward labor.

A clerk might have some opportunities to meet men, but the other jobs, not so much…

A maid? That's actually pretty hard work, and requires a decent amount of skill. Plus, there were very few chances to meet men other than colleagues and residents of the employer's house. Besides, my daily workload would be far too much to bear.

I wanted a job that allowed me to do as I pleased, and one that didn't require me to be too concerned about interpersonal relations, which meant self-employment was the best option.

First, I'll make ten tank-type potion containers and... No, that's the 'Self-Defense Force!'

"Anyway, after having learned important lessons from my previous mistakes, I've decided to go with this setup!" I declared in front of the city's entrance, to the group of unimpressed faces.

I continued my explanation anyway.

"First, our jobs... We will be running a normal shop."

"..." Roland and Francette gave me their best dubious expressions, apparently hung up on the "normal" part.

...*Shaddup!*

"It's not going to be a boxed lunch shop?" Belle asked, but...

"No, that's too much work. Far too much work for food that doesn't keep well. Pass!"

I did have the Item Box, but the meals degraded while they were on display, and doing the prep work every night and making lots of meals early in the morning was hell.

Francette, who I had forced to help us out in a tight spot, was obviously relieved.

"So, we'll be selling something other than food. Something that's easy to make, that doesn't spoil, and that doesn't require unnecessary hard work on our part!"

Selling things like general goods and ornaments would be so much easier. Especially when compared to a fish shop or a fruit and vegetable shop...

Everyone in the perishable foods industry, thank you for your hard work! No night-time prepping, early morning work, or kitchen work. Even if we didn't sell out our stock each day, we could just leave it on the shelves. We wouldn't need to store the items in the fridge or dispose of them. If we had to take time off out of nowhere, the business wouldn't be affected. No worries about food poisoning or food going bad either. And when I'm putting discount stickers on the stock before opening time, I wouldn't be harassed by a mob of old ladies to hurry up.

Hooray, non-food items!

"So, our story is that Layette, Belle, and I are sisters, and Emile is Belle's lover, who just recently became a hunter. Roland and Francette are a knightly couple, and they watch over us because they made an oath to our late parents. Francette might get away with it, but Roland's speech and mannerisms give him away as a noble, so he couldn't pass as our commoner brother. And Francette's a bit too young to be an elite common-born knight, so her backstory wouldn't work unless she was a noble. Besides, her equipment's a bit too nice for a commoner."

I decided not to make her Emile's sister because, well... If he and Belle started getting all lovey-dovey in public, people would think we're a family of weirdos, which would hurt my chances of finding a romantic partner. And if Francette and Belle were already taken, the young bachelors' attentions would naturally gravitate toward me.

Muahaha, it was the perfect plan!

...But if the men start paying attention to Layette instead of me, I'll cry!

"Okay then, let's do this!"

Nobody responded to my call, and they all moved their horses forward with their shoulders slumped.

Well, I wasn't expecting them to shout together or anything. The guards probably would've come running if they did. And of course, I had put the chariot back into my Item Box and was riding Ed, with Layette sitting in front of me. We moved forward at a casual pace toward the city.

This city wasn't the kind surrounded by walls, so everyone was free to enter and leave as they pleased. I wondered if they just weren't worried about enemy attacks, but then I realized this place was located off in a distant corner of the country, in a completely different direction from the capital, so it was highly unlikely an opposing faction would send their armies here. You can take down an opposing nation by taking their capital, so no idiot would waste their time taking an out-of-the-way location that wouldn't give them an advantage in battle.

Makes sense to me!

And since it was so far from the capital, I didn't have to worry about kings and princes bothering me, either. So, as long as I was careful with whatever lord ruled this place, I'd be totally fine…

…There was a time when I believed that.

"Huh? The king in this country is just a diplomatic ornament, and it's actually run by a council? It's not a real monarchy?"

According to Roland, this kingdom had a king and nobility, but the high-ranking nobles conducted meetings where they made all the important decisions, rather than the king doing it himself. And although it wasn't exactly a democracy or a republic, it was a bit different from other kingdoms and empires, since the voices of powerful commoners, especially the rich and important merchants, were quite influential.

"So I don't have to worry about lords and nobles here?"

"Of course you do! Lords are still lords, and nobles are still nobles. The nobles of this land are properly greedy and entitled and consider commoners to be nothing more than livestock, so don't worry."

Thought sooo!

Death Crimson!

I mean, King Crimson!

We were currently at the house—no, the shop we had signed a contract to rent.

Fortunately, all I needed to rent it was an up-front payment, and it didn't require any annoying certificates or guarantors. This wasn't the capital, but some out-of-the-way location off in the corner of the country, so the rent wasn't that high, despite it being a reasonably-sized town. The shop area of the building wasn't very big, but the living area was a decent size. After all, not only was I living with Emile and the others, but Roland and Francette would be joining as well.

I was going to have Emile and Belle share a room, and have Roland and Francette take another, but Francette adamantly refused, her face as red as a tomato.

"Wh-Wh-Wh-Whaaat?! An unmarried man and woman in the same room? You can't be serious!!!"

Huh? Whaaat?

"D-Don't tell me..."

Shocked, I glanced in the direction of Roland, who averted his eyes.

Ohhh... I had figured everyone but royalty and nobles in this world were loose about that sort of thing... Wait, Francette is a noble now! And she did say she had never dated a man before. Wait... So have they been staying in different rooms at the inns we stopped at all this time?

"When it comes to inns, we had to keep traveling expenses low, and I had my duty to protect him. That was work! This is different!"

I see... So she didn't mind staying in a camp or inn together, since it's part of her job as a knight, but when it comes to living in the same room, it's a different story...

What a pain!

On the other hand, Emile and Belle were acting as if being separated was out of the question, so I had them stay in the same room. I would be sharing my room with Layette, of course.

As for what this shop was going to be for...

"A utility shop?" everyone asked me.

Yes, it was going to be a 'utility shop.' The shop would be open from the first morning bell (6 a.m.) to the second morning bell (9 a.m.), then from the second daytime bell (3 p.m.) to the first evening bell (6 p.m.). It would only be open while everyone was leaving for work and coming back from work. I wasn't in dire need of money, so I didn't want to work more than was necessary. I'd rather use that time trying to find a marriage partner.

And for the products for our shop...

I pulled out the shelves and display stands we had used at Layette's Atelier from the Item Box and put them out in the shop area. And there, I placed the products I had picked out personally. Hard bread, jerky, cubes of dehydrated soup, dried vegetables and dried fruits. I would only be selling food that wouldn't spoil easily.

In addition, I laid out canteens, knives, capes, and hats for those who had sudden travel needs and had to buy some equipment. There were also spices, herbs, underwear, and even some disposable cosmetics. I added those emergency items little by little, from a broad range of categories.

"...Why would underwear and cosmetics be considered emergency items, you ask? Let's talk about that when Belle and Layette aren't here, Francette."

*   *

As soon as we arrived in the city, the first thing we did was secure a room at an inn. After that, we began gathering information from bored-looking people at the inn and the other guests staying there. Information was incredibly valuable, after all.

From what we gathered, merchants had a lot of rights in this country, and there was a merchant's association—in other words, a guild—that gathered taxes from other merchants and made payments to the government. So, in order to open a shop, we first needed to register with the Commerce Guild. I needed someone to introduce me to the right people if I was to rent out a shop anyway, so going to the guild and asking around was the fastest way to get what I wanted.

And so, I headed to the guild first thing in the morning, bringing Roland and Francette with me. After all, having adults with me would ensure that things went a lot smoother, rather than me going by myself, given that I looked like an underage child.

Francette looked to be 15 or 16 years old, so even though she was technically an adult, it wasn't quite enough to get by. That was why I had Roland tag along too. Anyone who saw Roland would assume correctly that he was an upper-class rich boy. Moreover, while wearing his sword, he cut something of an imposing figure.

As such, people would assume that Roland would hold the rights to the shop and be the shop owner, both in name only, while leaving the actual work to me and Francette. That was fine by me.

If a rumor went around about a child shopkeeper, a bunch of unwelcome types might have decided to come bug me. There are those who try to take from the weak in every world, after all. If an argument broke out, something terrible could happen... to the other party, that is.

I doubted Roland would be conscious of the danger posed to me or Francette, since he could just reveal his identity in a pinch and thus get out of trouble. And would Francette, Emile and Belle even think to go easy on someone who tried to cause me harm? I wouldn't show mercy to anyone who laid hands on Layette, after all. Absolutely not!

In any case... the fewer sources of conflict, the better. That's what it came down to.

"Excuse me, we'd like to open a new business..." I had asked for directions at the inn and, upon arrival at the Guild, spoke to the young reception girl at the desk.

"Oh... Y-Yes!" Yeah, she was looking right over my head and right at Roland's face...

Well, Roland was an ex-prince, after all, and he had the appearance to match. If he dressed up and rode in on a white horse, it'd be quite the regal picture. It wasn't so strange for a reception girl from a local city to swoon over him.

"...So, h-how may I help you?"

Th-This girl was too busy gawking at Roland to even listen to me! Wait, was Roland that popular with the ladies? Even without his royal title?

I looked over at Francette, who shrugged. Huh... So this happened pretty often.

"We! Would like! To open! A new business!!!"

"You don't have to shout! I can hear you!"

Shut it!

When I was an office worker, there was a time when I had to cover for the receptionists when they all fell ill with the flu. Though, for some reason, I was released from my duties in the middle of my first day... Anyway, a receptionist is the face of the company! When they don't put their all into their work...

Smack!

"Pardon me. I'd like to discuss your inquiry in detail, so please come right this way," a woman who was a little older than the first receptionist said, smiling, and guided us toward a separate meeting room.

"How mean! I was helping that handso— customer! You can't just come in and take... Hey, what are you doing?! Stop, I must help that handsome man..." The receptionist girl got her head smacked with rolled-up documents, then protested vigorously as her co-workers dragged her away.

Maybe this happened often, because they were pretty efficient in removing her. I was glad we didn't end up being assigned to that weirdo. Seriously...

"Well then. I am Irene, and I will be taking care of you today. I understand you are looking to open a new business. Please turn in a written request with the location, shop name, products handled and/or business form, as well as the size of your business. Your taxes and membership fees will be based on this information... Please note that if you report false information in an attempt to reduce the taxes owed, there will be issues later on..."

She finished her explanation quickly enough, but I wasn't even at that step yet.

"I'm sorry, but we still haven't worked out a location for our store. We came here hoping you could give us some guidance..."

"Oh, I see. Not to worry, there are quite a few people who do the same thing. This gives us an opportunity to collect a favor later from the estate agents for having referred you, and they also happen to be members of our guild."

I thought she would have gotten upset, but that wasn't the case at all. We were introduced to an estate agent, then we secured a store location, all thanks to the help of the guild.

After officially completing the registration process, I asked her something that was on my mind.

"Um, that receptionist we first talked to..."

"Oh, she's the granddaughter of our lord's nursemaid, so she won't get fired no matter what she does. She's not a bad girl... I suppose you could say she's honest, pure, true to her desires, or just unmannerly..."

That didn't sound like a good girl to me!

So, on the documents I submitted, I wrote:

Shop Location: Commercial Ward, 3rd Street
Products Handled: Anything
Business Size: 3 employees
Store Name: Belle

I didn't want to use the same shop name as last time, so I changed it up. The employees of record would be me, Belle, and Francette. I was going to have Belle train as a hunter with Emile again, but she would be helping out every so often, and I was afraid of being penalized for under-reporting, so I added her, just in case. It wasn't like I was hurting for money, and the difference in fees between two employees and three wasn't too different anyway.

I was planning on putting "Convenience Store Belle" on the sign. I wasn't going to call it a *conbini*. If I did, anyone who got transported here from Japan would immediately be able to tell some other Japanese person was already here. And what if that person made a move before me... Wait, what am I even fighting against?!

Anyway, preparations for shooting down UFOs—I mean, opening the shop—were complete! Now I just needed to order the sign! I had changed the shop name, so I couldn't reuse the old one.

...But first, I had to lay out the products and tell everyone about the shop.

*   *

And with the sign now complete, it was time to open the doors!

But it ended up being a quiet opening, since I hadn't really advertised at all. I wasn't planning on doing any heavy marketing. Honestly, I didn't want too many people coming in, and I wasn't selling anything particularly interesting anyway. Just a small shop where customers would occasionally stop by; that was what I wanted Convenience Store Belle to be.

This store was nothing more than a front to make it seem like my main source of income, after all. If word got out that I had a lot of money, enough to live comfortably on, it would attract the unsavory types and affect my search for a marriage partner. I wasn't interested in men who were after my wallet.

Plus, I needed something that would give me an opportunity to meet people. My mistake last time was thinking that I had to make money through my business. That had led to the idea that I needed good medicine to sell at a profit. I didn't need my business to be booming in order to find a man; I really only needed people to think I was just getting by with my shop.

Being in the red would be a bit much, though, so I would be satisfied with breaking even after living expenses, or making a slight profit. Big profits were completely unnecessary. Oh, maybe I could scrape up the costs for Ed's care too, though I didn't mind using my savings in the Item Box for that.

Emile and Belle were at the Hunter's Guild. They would likely just be introducing themselves and gathering info for today. They planned on taking on real tasks starting tomorrow.

Francette and Roland were relaxing in their rooms upstairs. They would come down in seconds if I rang the call bell, shouted for them, or pulled the string under the counter. So, for now, Francette could rest as much as she liked.

It was a far cry from keeping watch all day from the alley like last time. I felt bad for that. Really... Sorry about that...

I'd have Francette swap in for my breaks, but I would do the majority of the shopkeeping. Otherwise, it would defeat the purpose of running a shop to find a marriage partner. Layette would be there too, of course. Three-hour shifts, one in the morning and one in the afternoon. Six-hour workdays, with free time during the day. No late night prep work or early mornings.

Sold goods could be easily replenished as long as I had a few days' worth of stock stored in the Item Box. Ahh, this was a dream compared to the boxed meal shop or being a corporate slave like in my last life! I could even neglect my health and eat like crap and not worry about getting sick as long as I had my potions!

This is it! This is the life I've always wanteddd!!!

...Wait. If I got married, wouldn't I lose this dream life and have to make meals for my husband every day? If I had to deal with that, I might as well... No! No, no, no, no! Don't think about it! Don't think, just feel!

*　　*

Even without any advertising on my part, people came to check out the new shop out of sheer curiosity.

No one came in on the morning of the first day, but there were a decent number of locals and people coming home from work who stopped by in the evening. Ever since then, several people had started coming by, here and there, in the mornings and evenings alike.

"A 'convenient' store? You could find this stuff pretty much anywhere…"

When people pointed this out, I provided them with an explanation.

"It's true that these items can be found at other shops. Canteens at item shops, knives at blade shops, nonperishables at food stores, capes at clothing stores… But if you suddenly needed to travel someplace far away, you would need to stop by multiple stores to get all of those things, wouldn't you? And if you needed to leave first thing in the morning, you would have to wait until the second morning bell or first daytime bell to get them. But if you come here, you can get everything in one visit, and we open at the first morning bell! Wouldn't you say that's a convenient store?"

"Y-You're right…"

After hearing my explanation, most customers seemed to agree.

The prices for my wares weren't particularly cheap, but they weren't too high either. We put out a few things we liked, like cookies baked by yours truly, Belle's bamboo wares, and Emile's wood-carved animals, all sold at a very low price. As such, our run-of-the-mill shop, a shop that wasn't exactly thriving or in a horrible slump, quietly continued to do business.

*   *

"Hey mister, do you have anything weird in stock?"

"Weird, you say…?"

The shop is closed from the second morning bell (9 a.m.) to the second daytime bell (3 p.m.) This means that we have free time between those hours, but… I was getting a full eight hours of sleep—from 9 p.m. to 5 a.m.—so I couldn't really take a midday nap.

That's why I decided to go visit my supplier, taking Layette and Francette with me.

Roland said he was writing a letter to let his family know that he'd stayed safe during his travels… Wait, he was writing to the king! He was telling him about me, wasn't he?!

It wasn't like I was using my powers to make all of my wares. In fact, I had limited myself to using my powers exclusively for products I really wanted but was unable to get through normal means. Yes, I was buying most of my standard wares at other stores.

I still had plenty of money from what I had earned in Balmore, and I didn't want to disrupt the laws of the universe here… Though, I guess it was a bit too late for that. Anyway, this store was one of the places where I stocked up on general goods. It was a wholesale store, and it stocked a few interesting items once in a while, so I had to check in from time to time.

"How about this one? It's a specialty item from the faraway land of Aligot: a doll of the angel with scary-looking eyes."

"No, I don't want that!"

"If you collect all six, you'll be blessed by the angel with scary eyes…"

"Shut iiit!!!"

"Have you heard any other interesting things?"

My next stop was the Commerce Guild. As a merchant, I had to keep an ear open for news at all times.

"You were just here yesterday, Miss Kaoru... It's unusual to come by every day, you know. If we get any urgent news or information that could greatly affect business, we'll send a runner to alert the guild members."

But I was bored! So bored! I needed to do *something* to keep me occupied! It seemed that having a lot of free time had its disadvantages. It'd been nearly five years and my corporate slave mentality still hadn't left me! Damn it...

I was lying around at home a lot back in Balmore when I lived with the Eyes of the Goddess, but with all the potion stuff, development of new products with the Abili Trade Company, providing sailing technology to the Aligot Empire, and dealing with other countries, I had kept pretty busy...

Anyway, it was time for my evening shift.

Finding myself bored each day, I was beginning to wonder if I had made a mistake. I had done all that yearning for a safe and peaceful life, sure, but once it became a reality, it was just so unexciting. And to be honest, I wasn't in that big of a rush to get married either. If I wasn't going to get any older, maybe I could travel the world and enjoy myself for a while. At least for a little while longer, I could live how I pleased... I could always settle down somewhere and have kids later...

I was daydreaming thoughts like those, when...

"Excuse me, do you have any hemort seeds?"

Hemort? I'd never heard of it, but it must come from a plant, considering that it's a seed. The girl was around 16-17 years old, with a look of half-desperation and half-resignation. She was considered an adult by this world's standards, but seeing the young girl's face, a thought crossed my still-hazy mind.

How can I call this a "convenience store" if I can't provide a customer with something they really need?

My mind had been up in the clouds for so long, it took awhile for the cogs in my head to start turning. So, I decided to just hurry up and give her what she wanted.

...A double-layered container with a potion in the bottom half and hemort seeds in the top half!

I made a container appear in my hand under the counter, then I placed it on the counter.

"Here you go, hemort seeds."

I didn't know what kind of plant a hemort was, but this would probably do. I had to believe in the Goddess's factory. The seed looked like a soybean, but I figured it was completely different. There were about 20 of them.

I couldn't give her the healing potion, so I only gave her the contents of the top half of the container.

How much should I charge her...

"Wh-Whaaat? T-They really are hemort seeds..."

She was flabbergasted. I thought that's what she wanted?

"I-I didn't think you'd actually have them..."

It seemed she wasn't expecting much in the first place. Don't take the "convenience store" lightly.

It's just a vegetable seed...

Though, to be fair, I didn't actually have it in stock.

Well, it was almost time for the first night bell, so the other stores had been closed for a while already. Maybe she was a farmer's daughter, and she was going back to the country tonight or first thing in the morning.

"Th-Then, do you have a mortgul fruit or a kurcul leaf?

Hmm, maybe pulling everything out from under the counter would be a bit suspicious.

"One moment, please."

With that, I went into the storage room, which was about the size of a closet...

"Double-layered containers with healing potions in the bottom compartment, with a mortgul fruit in the top layer of one container and a kurcul leaf in the other!"

It struck me that the mortgul fruit thing could've been the size of a watermelon, coconut, or durian...but it was only the size of a piece of gum.

Whew!

I removed the upper compartment of each container and brought them over to the counter.

"Here you go, a mortgul fruit and a kurcul leaf."

Huh? She's not moving...

"Wh-Wh-Wha…"

The girl was stricken with even greater shock than earlier, before finally coming back to reality.

"Wh-Why is this heeere?!"

What kind of question was that…?

"Because we're a convenience store!"

Yes, this was the only answer I could give in this situation. This shop is convenient, hence the name.

Even if the other shops were closed, and regardless of the fact that we weren't a specialty seed store… We sell that stuff here, and that's why we're so convenient! Muahahaha!

"So, h-how much will it be…?"

Oh. This was bad. I didn't know the market price. But it was just a vegetable seed, a small fruit, and a leaf. How pricey could it possibly be?

If a customer thought I was trying to rip them off, it could destroy my business. So…

"That will be six small silver coins."

Yeah, that should do it.

Two small silver coins each, equivalent to about 600 Japanese yen. That shouldn't be too much.

Why did she look like it was the end of the world? Was six small silver coins really so much? Did she actually come shopping without 600 yen worth of money?!

"I-I'm sorry, I don't have quite enough on me right now, but I'll definitely be back tomorrow! So please, accept this as payment for now!"

With that, the girl removed the pendant around her neck and gently placed it on the counter.

…Wait, this was definitely worth more than six small silver coins. In fact, its value was probably off by two, no, maybe even *three* digits…

But seriously, why was she running around town trying to do emergency shopping without even six small silver coins on her?

Oh, while I was standing there in shock, the girl had shoved the three containers into her pocket and ran off.

This wasn't theft… was it? Maybe she took my silence as acceptance. Like that saying, "If you have no objections, answer with silence." Or maybe she was in such a hurry that she couldn't even wait for an answer…

Oh well, it wasn't a big deal. She would likely be back tomorrow to retrieve the pendant, hopefully with six small silver coins this time…

* *

"Excuse me!"

"You are not excused!"

"Wha…?" a girl and an old man said as they stood in the entrance, mouths agape.

"Oh, uh, never mind! Welcome!"

The pendant girl from yesterday and an elderly man with a white beard entered the shop.

"I am Oredeim, an apothecary. I understand this girl visited your establishment yesterday. I would like to purchase her pendant back from you. That was her late mother's keepsake…"

What the heck, why was he looking at me like I was the bad guy?! She was the one who left it because she couldn't pay six measly small silver coins…

In any case, I took the pendant from under the counter and placed it on the counter. Seeing this, the old man produced a pouch from his chest pocket and reached into it for some coins.

"I understand this is business, but to take advantage of her like this..." he said, placing the six coins on the counter.

Huh? Did he really go that far over six small silver coins? The glass containers that held the seeds and leaves cost more than that... Wait, hold up!

"What is this?! You've got some nerve trying to pawn off counterfeit money, geezer!"

"Huh?"

"Whaa?"

A guy like this deserved to be called a geezer... The girl was brazenly acting as if she was surprised, but even I knew the currency of this country, foreigner or not. It wasn't as if I had just opened up yesterday.

So, it was glaringly obvious that the objects on the table weren't small silver coins... And it goes without saying that they weren't silver coins, gold coins, or small gold coins either.

"If you can't even pay six small silver coins, fine. Just take that and go. I don't want you stepping foot in this shop again. You're banned!"

With that, I pushed the pendant and counterfeit coins on the table toward them.

"Whaaaaaat?!" they yelled in unison.

What were they so surprised about? They couldn't have expected to fool me with those fake coins...

Then, looking a bit shaken, the geezer said, "Umm... Those are mithril coins, not counterfeit small silver coins..."

Wha?

He explained that the 6 coins here were "mithril coins," and as the name implied, they were coins mainly made of mithril, with each one being worth 10 gold coins.

…Which made each one equivalent to about a million Japanese yen.

I mean, I knew *of* the existence of mithril coins. But I'd never actually seen one in person. It wasn't used by the commoners, and I heard that they were only really used among the nobility, or in religious ceremonies.

It wasn't that they were particularly hard to acquire, but most people only needed to use gold coins. Mithril coins were hard to use because of their high value, and since they weren't commonly seen, most people didn't have the ability to discern between real ones and fakes. So, you'd normally use 60 gold coins rather than 6 mithril coins.

60 gold coins wouldn't even weigh 500 grams, and they weren't particularly cumbersome to carry around. They assumed I had asked for 6 mithril coins, so they went through the trouble of exchanging 60 gold coins for 6 mithril ones.

Wait, wait, wait, wait, waaait! How the heck did 600 yen turn into 6,000,000 yen?!

Th-This was bad… My hands were shaking… Oh no, I accidentally hit the hand bell for calling Francette and Emile, and it fell to the floor…

"You will pay for your crimes with your blood, scoundrel!"

Francette and Emile's blades were pressed against the old man's neck. At the same time, Roland's sword and Belle's knife were held to the girl's neck. They were completely frozen in place, faces pale and sweat erupting from their faces.

*   *

"...So, when I said 'six small silver coins,' you thought I meant 'six mithril coins,' and tried to pay that amount."

"Th-That's right!"

Afterwards, I hurriedly got everyone to put their weapons away, switched the "Open" sign to "Be Back Soon," then took everyone upstairs. I gave the pendant and mithril coins back to the little girl and the old man, respectively, for now. And after I had questioned them, the girl began to explain her situation, with desperation in her expression.

"But there's no way hemort seeds, mortgul fruits, and kurcul leaves could be bought for six small silver coins! This time of year, even low-quality varieties would cost twenty gold coins, and could be up to forty gold coins if they were of high quality! How could I not think you meant mithril coins when you mumbled six silver coins?!"

"Indeed, I would have assumed that she was a crooked merchant, and was trying to take advantage of you, if that was the case. That is a million times more likely than believing some mad merchant put an absurd price like six small silver coins on such rare items!"

The girl and old man took turns making their point.

Hearing this, Roland and Francette held their heads in their hands.

Then, staying in that position, Francette let out a groan and asked, "Umm... Kaoru, do you know what hemort seeds, mortgul fruits, and kurcul leaves are used for, where and when they're produced, or their market prices?"

"... No..."

The old man immediately took out his pouch, pulled out six small silver coins, then placed them on the table.

"Well, we'll be heading out now!"

With that, he took the bewildered girl by her arm and rose, preparing to leave.

"Now hold on just a minute!" Francette, Roland, and I cried out, raising our voices all at once.

They were used to this reaction by now...

And so we stopped the old man and the girl from leaving the six silver coins and taking off.

"I paid the price you asked for. I see no problem here!"

I couldn't argue with that...

"I asked for your price, and paid appropriately. Are you telling me this shop is in the habit of raising its prices *after* selling its products and then charging additional fees to its customers?"

"Uuu..." we all moaned, quietly.

A valid point. I just needed some tea to calm myself down. It would have to be ceylon tea, of course... Wait, shut up!

"But that's a bit too..."

"It's fine, Fran," I stopped Francette as she began to retort.

Then...

"You're absolutely right. This was a business transaction, after all."

"Y-Yes, exactly. I'm glad you seem to understand..."

The old man seemed to calm down a bit upon seeing my smiling face. Oredeim the apothecary, was it?

"So, I'll just take the six small silver coins, as per the price I quoted originally. But since I won't be able to explain the sale at such a price to my supplier, and because I want to avoid a situation in which you ask for the same price again, or even others who have heard about this incident requesting the same thing, I will have to return all of my remaining plant-based ingredients and stop carrying them altogether. Therefore, if anyone comes in requesting

69

such products from here on, I will have to refuse the sale, after explaining what transpired here in great detail."

"What?!"

Yes, this was convenient for me too. This way, I could avoid this place being known as a shop that carries valuable ingredients and sells them for dirt cheap. I was glad the old man decided to take up the attitude he did. My overhead cost for those items was zero anyway, so it wasn't like my wallet was going to suffer.

"You still have remaining stock?!"

…Huh? That's what he was concerned about? I thought he would change his mind and want to pay the six mithril coins instead. Don't tell me he planned on buying up the rest for cheap, too… What if he started claiming, 'You said they were six silver coins!'?

Oh man… No way would I put up with that. But saying there was still remaining stock was my critical mistake. How could I get through this…

Then, all at once, I had it.

"Of course, it's not here, at this particular moment. The stock is stored in a different building, one that has the appropriate humidity and temperature. The seeds may be fine for dry storage, but fruits and leaves are delicate, after all. Normal vegetables, seeds, and fruits are also stored there, so when I ordered products in bulk, some expensive ones must have been mixed in with my order. The person I put in charge of ordering and separating the products must have made a mistake, and since I don't have in-depth knowledge of such goods, well… Assuming they were common products, I priced them on a whim, which was my mistake… Anyway, I'll be returning everything in the storage area too, so those items won't be stocked here in the future."

There, that just explained why I don't have stock here, and why the price ended up being so ridiculous the last time. Peace at my shop had been preserved!

"Wha… Th-Then, you won't be restocking…?"

"I will not. Besides, I wouldn't want to continue selling high-priced items to a customer who demands to buy those goods at an absurdly cheap price, fully aware that it was the result of a pricing error. It's far too risky for me, considering that you could use some careless mistake or comment as a lever to make another such purchase, losing us dozens of gold coins in the process. Honestly, it's hard to believe that you've taken up such an exploitative attitude with us if you intended on doing business with us in the future. What, did you think I'm an idiot?"

Well… I mean, I was pretty aloof and stupid that first time…

"What?! But I didn't think you had more stock…"

"So you took advantage of my mistake and tried to buy it for *one-ten-thousandth* of the market price, right? You got it for the price you wanted. Congratulations. While you only had to give up a small amount of money for this sale, you also lost the most crucial element for anyone who deals with other people on a regular basis: confidence and trust. But I'm sure you're well aware of that."

The old man seemed quite flustered.

For me, though, I had to avoid people thinking that this shop had valuable goods for sale at all costs, so I had to make it clear that those items would never be available here again. It wasn't as if the old man was losing access to something he had been getting here regularly, anyway. He just so happened to acquire something that was already hard to get. I'm sure it wasn't a big deal if he continued to have trouble finding it, and even if it was an issue, it wasn't one that concerned me.

"And you?" I asked the girl who had been watching all of this happen.

She seemed nervous to be called out so suddenly.

"Huh? M-Me? I-I'm the master's disciple, Taona..."

The old man had called himself an apothecary, so I thought there was a chance she could have been his client, but he had spoken on the girl's behalf earlier, so I guess she was with him after all. So, she was just as guilty... I mean, she hadn't really done anything wrong, but she *was* this jerk's companion...

"I suppose we are done here..."

"W-Wait! I may be the only one in this city who knows how to make Longevity Medicine! You wouldn't want to lose a regular customer..."

"Regular customer? You mean the first-timer who only paid six silver coins? The one who profited off of us losing nearly forty gold coins, at that?"

"Urgh... But, for our transactions from here on out..."

"Here on? We are no longer handling plant-based ingredients. Do you intend on buying enough portable foods and daily wares to earn us forty gold coins in profits?"

The old man closed his mouth.

"Our customers are leaving now. Francette, Emile, please see them out."

"Right away!"

"Yes, ma'am!" Francette and Emile responded, expressions serious.

They seemed to be happy to be doing bodyguard-like work for the first time in a while. But they were just kicking out a tired old man and a helpless little girl, so it wasn't all that knightly of a task...

Mainly, I figured they were glad to get an order from me and sort of reconfirm their place and sense of purpose here. Belle looked regretful about not being chosen for the task, but she was just as weak as the two we were kicking out.

Emile ignored the girl, who was closer to him, and approached the old man. It seemed he had reservations about laying hands on and using force with a young girl, and so, Francette went with her instead.

I hoped they wouldn't break any bones by accident.

"Unhand me, I'm not done talking here! Who do you think I am...?"

The old man resisted and was dragged out of the room by Emile, while the girl simply followed after them, without Francette needing to touch her at all.

I was exhausted...

But, thanks to the old man's attitude, I was able to play off my mistake of selling some odd products for a horribly abnormal price. Now it was like that 'mysterious triple plant set' never existed. Good.

...So, what the heck is Longevity Medicine?

*   *

I explained the whole ordeal to the others after we'd kicked out the two guests. When I told them, "I handled it, so now everything's a-okay!" Roland and Francette gave me an incredulous look.

But Emile and Belle were nodding in agreement...

"...There's no way that's the end of it," Roland muttered quietly, and Francette nodded in response.

Why?

"Francette, what's Longevity Medicine?"

I was talking about the medicine that the old apothecary guy, Oredeim, had mentioned.

He had said he might be the only person in the city who could make it, so it must have been quite valuable. It also likely meant that the old man was very skilled. He must've been, if he was one of the top apothecaries around, although this was just a provincial city. His haughty attitude made it all the more likely, too.

"Kaoru, you don't even know that...? Well, I suppose it's not your fault. It has nothing to do with the Goddess, and you wouldn't need anything like that, since you can make the Tears of the Goddess. And you're not the Goddess of this world in the first place..."

She was right.

Then Francette straightened her back and began explaining the situation to me with a serious look on her face.

Apparently, she was in 'normal mode' earlier, and her explanation would now be carried out in 'work mode.'

"Longevity Medicine is, as the name implies, medicine that's said to prolong one's life. Its method of creation is passed down from master to disciple, and it's often mentioned in old stories, too. It's said to use all sorts of rare ingredients, cure all sorts of ailments, and extend one's lifespan..."

"But, in reality, it's just normal medicine," Roland said, interrupting Francette.

"Wha...?" Francette and I trailed off, gaping.

Francette is surprised too?!

"It's not that it doesn't work. It's very effective for certain ailments, and if given to someone who's on the verge of death, it'll even slightly increase their chances of survival. So it's true that some people have been saved and lived longer thanks to Longevity Medicine, and it's understandable why it's so sought after, even when it goes for an extremely high price. It certainly isn't foolish to do so. But this isn't a magical drug that cures all ailments, or the medicine of the gods. Just an expensive and effective medicine. It's not anything like Kaoru's potions. Word of Kaoru's potions has probably only reached the top officials around here, so most people would think of Longevity Medicine if they were asked what the ultimate medicine is."

Huh, so it was like ginseng in the Edo period. Ginseng later became available for wealthier commoners too, but in places like China and Korea, only the emperor, royals, and nobles could purchase it, and in Japan's case, it was only accessible for the shoguns, daimyo, and powerful families. I wouldn't be surprised if something like that was worth millions of yen.

But instead of a magical elixir that could immediately cure all symptoms upon consumption, it made the user more healthy over time, gradually improving their condition... So instead of curing your symptoms and thus making you healthy, it makes you healthy, so the symptoms are eventually cured. Kind of like vitamins and nutrients.

"And the price is so high because those three plants are essential ingredients, but they're also hard to obtain. They can only be harvested in distant countries, and they're hard to come by because they can't be cultivated. The hemort seeds are one thing, but the mortgul fruits and kurcul leaves can only be harvested during certain seasons, and their effectiveness declines sharply when they're dried out… and Kaoru sold all three of them, fresh, for six small silver coins total. Mortgul fruits can't be harvested this time of year, by the way. They likely ran low on hemort seeds and were searching high and low for more, and although they were unlikely to find them here, they stopped by, without really expecting anything, because we handle plant-based products here. When the girl found out we had them, she must have asked about the mortgul fruit and kurcul leaves as a kind of joke. The ones they have must be dried and low-quality. But you…"

Gah! I'd made a terrible mistake. I couldn't be mad at Taona for mistaking 'six small silver coins' for 'six mithril coins.' She was expecting to be quoted a ridiculously high price, so it was natural to hear it the way she did.

I've experienced something similar myself. And that Oredeim guy didn't seem to blame Taona for her mistake. This all could've been avoided if she just paid the six silver coins and pretended not to notice anything. He probably couldn't have blamed her then, either.

Well, that may have been the case this time, but I probably would have looked up the market price for next time, so I would've found out about the appropriate pricing eventually. But I would have been upset about her not mentioning the fact that the price was ridiculously low, and upset at myself for selling such a thing so carelessly, and removed that type of product from our inventory. So, in the end, the result would've been the same.

But…

"Why do you know so much about Longevity Medicine, Roland? You even know about the ingredients… I thought only a select few apothecaries know about it?"

I was curious as to why he was so knowledgeable on the subject. It was almost as if he could mix it himself.

"I was forced to take it. For a long time, too, after I was injured and I couldn't move my arm. I insisted there was no point in taking it, because I wasn't weakened by any kind of sickness, but my parents and retainers wouldn't listen. To think, how much of the kingdom's funds they wasted... So, I intently questioned the apothecaries and researched everything there is to know about the medicine, all to convince everyone that it was pointless to take it for my injury."

Wow. I felt bad for asking. He probably couldn't allow himself to waste funds that were supposed to be used for the people. It must have been a painful memory for him.

"...Sorry."

Roland waved his hand lightly, telling me not to worry about it. But my question had been answered, and I found out that this Longevity Medicine wasn't all that it's cracked up to be. Case closed!

I had a little too much free time here, but it was way better than abandoning everything and running away. All I needed was a decent number of customers and a steady income. And meeting people! That was all I was asking for!

Honestly, though, I wasn't in any kind of rush. My body wouldn't get any older, so I didn't need to worry about being a suitable age for marriage. Francette and the others probably assumed I was tens of thousands of years old anyway, so a few more years weren't going to change anything.

50,019 years old, 50,024 years old... It didn't matter. Maybe I could even travel around some, then return to Balmore once I was done, and have Francette and Roland marry. While I'm at it, have Emile and Belle get married, and maybe find Layette a husband, too. Then I could go on a solo adventure from there...

Actually, going on a journey with just Layette might be better. Then I could depart right away, without waiting around too long. Being alone would be a bit lonely.

When we get back to Balmore, I can always find an Aligot ship at some port town and hop on... There was a time when I thought about things like that.

*   *

"Is this the place that sells materials for the Longevity Medicine?!"

Here we go! Why did they come at all?! I clearly told that old man that I wouldn't be restocking any more of those ingredients...

Besides, there shouldn't have been any reason for him to tell anyone else about them. How annoying...

"No, it isn't. Please look elsewhere."

"But this is Convenience Store Belle, is it not?!"

Hmm... He seemed like a nobleman's middle-aged retainer, or maybe a rich merchant's protégé, but where had he heard about this...? I needed to confirm that first to figure out how to proceed.

I had to find out what he did and didn't know, or I could end up giving him unnecessary information and making things worse.

But first...

pull, pull

I gave the string under the counter a few light tugs, in a specific rhythm.

The string was for calling Francette, who was relaxing upstairs. Pulling the string would ring the bell in everyone's rooms and make their lights blink. We had a system so that information could be relayed by the number of and intervals between the blinking lights. The signal this time indicated, "Urgency level: four, threat level: four, number of people: 1."

This should be low enough that she would come down the stairs normally instead of skipping three steps at a time...

thud thud thud thud thud!

Never mind.

Emile and Belle were out for hunter training and earning money. They tried to give me all of their earnings, but I only accepted half of what they made and stored their wages in a container inside the Item Box for when they got married.

Roland was out somewhere, so he was also absent. It wasn't as if he was cooped up in his room all day, every day. I sometimes went out with Francette while Emile and Belle were home. So, that left...

"You there! Prepare yourself!"

Yup, just Francette.

"Francette, the signal was for urgency level four and threat level four..."

But that didn't matter to Francette. In her eyes, everything was either harmless or a serious potential danger to me. It was one or the other, and she would face the latter with full force, regardless of how low the threat appeared to be. And the thought of handling things in a controlled or peaceful manner never really occurred to her.

Yeah, I knew that.

"Wha..." The middle-aged man cringed in surprise.

It was only natural, considering he had only gone out shopping and now he had an armed swordswoman pointing her blade at him. Maybe he was planning on leading up to threats and the use of force, but we weren't quite there yet, and he probably didn't expect a guard at a small store like this one. That explained why he came alone, despite having that high-handed attitude.

Judging by how he couldn't react coherently to Francette's sword, I could tell he wasn't very strong... But compared to Francette, most people would probably fall into that category. But now I could take my time and calmly get the information I wanted.

*   *

"So, you're saying the child of this Baron Dorivell is in danger..."

"D-Don't say such nonsense out loud!"

The middle-aged man, the one who had denied my words while getting all flustered, introduced himself as the knightly retainer of the baronial family.

Well, it wasn't as if all knights had to be young and handsome. They could accomplish feats in their youth and leave the field for a managerial position, eventually ending up with a big belly and bald head. The passage of time can be a cruel thing indeed...

"But isn't that what you just said? Besides, unless this is the crown prince we're talking about, you wouldn't use such a medicine unless he was dying, right?"

I'd already learned about this stuff from Roland. You know, just in case.

"B-Be that as it may, what if your careless, inappropriate comments reach someone's ears?! There is a big difference between being in poor health and being in danger!"

Ah, he was right... Especially when it came to the son and heir of a noble family, such rumors spreading around could lead to internal trouble, or worse. I was in the wrong here.

"...I'm sorry."

I had no choice but to apologize. And by apologizing, my mistake was wiped clean. It was my turn to go on the offensive again.

"So, where and how did you hear about these rare medicine ingredients being sold here?"

It could only be that old man, but conjecture and confirmation were very different things. Plus, I had to find out just how much he had revealed.

"I'm sure you've guessed by now, but I heard from Oredeim, the apothecary. The baron heard the child of a merchant family had taken this Longevity Medicine, and threa— convinced the merchant to tell him where he obtained it. He found out the merchant had requested Oredeim, who obtained the highest-quality materials for eighty gold coins, and thus made him the medicine for a hundred gold coins. Then, the baron prayed for the safety of Oredeim and his disciple, and for some reason, he revealed the source of his materials, despite resisting so much at first... By the way, Oredeim said to tell you, 'If you're going to that store, please tell her I didn't want to tell you where I obtained the ingredients,' so there you are."

...I didn't know where to begin. First of all, that damned geezer! He was up-charging like crazy!! Roland had told me that medicine's price mostly came from the cost to obtain those three ingredients. The other ingredients were far more reasonably priced, and comparatively easy to obtain. Which means... He was charging eighty gold coins for something he acquired for six small silver coins. Plus, a twenty-gold fee on top just to make it! Dirty old geezer...

Wait, but maybe this was a good thing? The price he'd sold his medicine for had no effect on me, and maybe this was far better than him blabbing about buying the ingredients for six small silver coins... That price was less suspicious, considering the time of year and the quality of the goods, and considering the high price, resellers wouldn't be tempted to flock here, even if the source was leaked to the general public.

Had the geezer actually done a good job? If so, then there was no need for me to go out of my way to tell them I sold the ingredients for six silver coins… Wait, that must have been that geezer's plan all along!

"Has he informed you we no longer carry them here?"

"He has. However, you were able to obtain the items at such a high quality before… It should be possible for you to use the same route to get more. Please, I beg of you. Help us, for the sake of Master Challotte…"

I was surprised. This proud-looking, portly, middle-aged man, a man who served a noble family, was bowing his head to some girl like me…

But at the same time, I was conflicted. I would have treated him coldly if he had come in here acting all high-and-mighty and trying to order me around, but I couldn't just turn down a nice, middle-aged man lowering his head to a little girl for the sake of his master's son.

Urrrgh…

Francette saw my struggle and gave me an exasperated look. Damn it Francette, aren't you a protector of middle-aged men too?! Well, she did admire Roland, so pretty princes and young knights were probably more her type. She still didn't understand how good the grizzled ones are. So young…

Wait, now's not the time to be thinking about this!

Hmm…

But there was only one answer I could give…

"I no longer have access to that connection. When we decided to stop selling plant-based items as a consequence of this particular case, I had my connection change their location, so that I could avoid a situation where a person of power could pressure me into giving up that information. So, even if I were to send an order now, it would just get sent back to me, as there would be no one to receive it. I wouldn't be able to find them, either. Also, I've already told them that if someone tried reaching out using my name, it would be an imposter faking my identity, so it would be best to make an excuse to cut contact, or assume it's coming from scoundrels who had threatened or tortured me, and act accordingly."

He let out an exclamation of surprise at hearing about my thorough preparation. As for Francette, she was giving me a suspicious look. I'd have thought she was used to my top-of-the-head remarks by now...

"S-So, the ingredients for the medicine..."

"Will never be stocked again, as the apothecary has told you. There is also no way for me to restock them, even if I wanted to. This store won't be handling any medical supplies other than common medicine, bandages, and the like. This is just a 'convenience store' for supplying basic goods on short notice, and it's our policy to leave any professional-grade items to their respective specialty stores..."

This should have gone without saying. What sort of convenience store would be better stocked than a specialty store?! But the man's dejected and disquieted look was hard to see. It would've been easier if he flew into a rage and started yelling. The guilt was starting to get to me...

But if I told him I could get the items, it would be the same result as last time. I couldn't allow that to happen. Even if the man was giving me an imploring look, like a rain-soaked chihuahua...

Urrrgh!

"...Kaoru, is there nothing you can do for him?" Francette suddenly spoke up, and the man's eyes lit up at the unexpected support.

Why would you shoot your ally in the back at a time like this, Fran?

It was pointless to think about.

"Just ask, and they'll sell you rare materials."

If such a rumor got around, it would all be over. Even if I insisted on keeping this a secret, what if another member of the baron's family got sick, like his wife or his daughter?

What about other noble dependents? Their families? A retainer close to the baron, or the baron's family? What if an upper-class noble above them asked for it? What if their kin ordered it? I suspected the chance of him keeping a promise to stay quiet, a promise that he made with some commoner girl, at that, was zero. The only possible option was to have him give up and leave.

"I'm sorry, but there is nothing I can do."

And so, the man plodded away, wearily. What's that judging look for, Francette?!

"...And that's what happened."

After our meal, I explained what happened to the others. I mean, if I had brought up that story while eating, it would have made the food taste bad. I had to wait until we were done.

"Francette, you..."

Roland gave Francette an exasperated look. Emile and Belle looked at Francette reproachfully.

"N-No, I didn't give her a judging look... That's just how Kaoru took it. This is a false accusation!"

Francette desperately tried to explain herself. However...

"But you were looking at me just like that!"

With that, I pointed at Emile and Belle, who were looking at Francette, and Francette looked down in shame.

"...I'm sorry. I couldn't help but remember the time I brought Lord Hector and Lady Yunith to their grandmother after she had fallen ill..."

Francette was talking about Earl Adan's family, who she had served before serving Roland. The air in the carriage with those four—the siblings, the maid, and Francette—must have been quite heavy before she received the potion from me.

Francette was too kind for her own good to begin with. She couldn't just abandon someone who she had the ability to help... assuming that someone wasn't considered an enemy by her, her friends, or me, that is.

This time, I saw anyone who wanted me to do something that could draw the attention of the rich and powerful as being my enemy, but that wasn't the case for Francette. Well, she wanted me to be worshiped by the people as a goddess, so I supposed she was all for having me do goddess-like deeds. But with Roland trying to interfere with me finding a marriage partner, and Francette trying to get me to show off my goddess powers and draw attention...

I had enemies all around me! What the hell!!

"Emile, Belle. I have a divine order for you two, as members of the Eyes of the Goddess."

"Yes!" they replied, earnestly.

Whenever I spoke with a formal and serious attitude like this, it meant I wasn't messing around. They would take it as an absolute order. Therefore, I had to be very careful about the exact orders I gave out. Otherwise, they would put their lives on the line, even if it was something dumb.

"You are to find out more about that visitor's master, the so-called Baron Dorivell, and his son, Challotte. However, you must prioritize your safety above all else while conducting your investigation. My servants are millions of times more important to me than the child of some unknown noble. Should you be careless with your own lives, you would be looking down upon and putting my servants in danger. Your lives belong to me. I will not allow you to die without my permission!"

Since that time at the well, this was the second time I had told them they weren't allowed to die without my permission.

Emile and Belle replied energetically, then ran out the door.

"M-Me too!"

Francette tried to follow, but I grabbed her by the arm.

"Not you, Francette."

"Wh-Why...? I-I want a divine order too..."

Ah... 'A knight who had taken up a divine order.' Sounded like a title Francette would die for.

"M-Me either?"

I turned around to find Roland standing there. Right... Come to think of it, he really, really wanted that divine sword. Maybe Roland had a lot of admiration for those things, too...

"No. Those two have done these sorts of jobs in the past, so they're used to it. You two have combat abilities that are far greater than theirs, but gathering information about someone without being caught isn't your forte. Besides, you two stand out way too much."

Francette and Roland couldn't argue back, and just slumped their shoulders. I felt a little bad for them...

"Okay, then. Francette, massage my shoulders! That is my divine order!"

"Y-Yes, ma'am!"

I meant it as a joke, but Francette pounced on the opportunity. She swiftly came up behind me and...

"Gyaaa! Ow ow owww!"

Forgetting to curb her strength out of excitement, Francette squeezed my shoulders with a vice-like grip.

"Gyaaa!"

Then, Layette leaped forth and bit Francette's neck to protect me. That was the only exposed part of her skin while attacking from behind.

"Gyaaaaaa! Gwaaaaaah!!!"

Francette instinctively squeezed my shoulders harder from the pain and surprise of being bitten. Then, she swung her body around in an attempt to get Layette off of her, making Layette's teeth sink into her neck even deeper. Layette clung onto Francette, continuing to bite as if her life depended on it. Francette crushed my shoulders with an even stronger grip.

"Gyaaaaaaaaagh!!!"

It was a scene straight from a nightmare...

"Haah... Haah... Haah..." we all panted, winded.

The look in Roland's eyes as he stared down at the three of us, laying on the ground and exhausted, was painful to see...

*   *

"Reporting the results of our investigation…"

Once evening rolled around, Emile and Belle came home. According to them, Baron Dorivell had one boy and two girls. They had been born in the order of 'boy, girl, girl,' and they were ten, seven, and five years old, respectively. Challotte, the boy that the servant had mentioned, was the eldest son.

No wonder he seemed so desperate…

Well, not that he would have put any less effort into it if he had another successor lined up. Besides, the baron's wife wasn't too old to have more children… but I guess that didn't matter to a parent who cared for their child.

In any case, this Challotte was the only boy in the Dorivell house. And he was in critical condition, due to his illness…

"Baron Dorivell is Rank B. The Challotte boy is Rank B Plus. Of course, this is based solely on rumors from outside sources…"

Oho, those are pretty high ranks.

These "ranks" were a rating system the Eyes of the Goddess had used when I was in the Kingdom of Balmore, mainly to determine whether the target was worth saving.

"C" meant they were average nobles, not particularly good nor bad.

"D" meant that they were somewhat bad nobles.

"E" meant that they were garbage.

"B" meant they were pretty good for nobles, and "A" was reserved for the very good ones.

These five levels also had plus and minus variants, leaving a total of fifteen ranks.

There were exceptions to the rule, of course, but a Rank B adult and a Rank B Plus child were well within the range for being worthy of receiving the goddess's mercy.

"All right, it's time for phase two of the investigation. I want you to keep it up tomorrow."

This is the first task I've given them in my role as the angel since we left Balmore.

Oh, and I'd given up on claiming I wasn't the angel long ago. There was no point in continually repeating myself, and if I brought it up, I risked Francette claiming I was a goddess instead of an angel.

"Thank you, Lady Kaoru…"

Francette usually just called me Kaoru, but when there were no outsiders around and the topic was related to the angel or goddess, she addressed me as Lady Kaoru. I figured there wasn't much that could be done about that, and let her do as she pleased.

"I'm not doing this because you wished for it, Francette. I'd already decided to continue saving people back when I left Balmore. And the one granting salvation to the people is the Angel, and not the girl known as Kaoru, who runs Convenience Store Belle, so there's no problem there!"

"Lady Kaoru…" Francette stared at me with a look of reverence, but she had always worshiped me in the first place, so that was business as usual.

Add ninety-degree water to water that's ninety degrees, and it'd remain ninety degrees. That was just how she was.

Now, how should I handle this job…

Chapter 32:
Work

"I am a potion maker from another land. My potions have been consumed in royal courts."

I said as such to the gate guards, and they greeted me with the utmost courtesy. I was even wearing a suspicious-looking mask to disguise myself.

...Should they really be letting such a sketchy person inside so easily?!

When I asked, one of them responded, "If something were to happen, you and I would simply lose our heads. Compared to the possibility of Master Challotte recovering from his illness, such an outcome is of no consequence."

'No consequence,' my butt! I'd like to keep my head, thank you!

But to think that even the guard could say such a thing with confidence... They really must have been good nobles. Emile and Belle's report must have been right. I wasn't doubting the accuracy of their reports, of course.

And so, one of the guards led me into the manor. This was, needless to say, the residence of the Dorivell baronial family. I had heard they were looking for doctors and medicine, regardless of their social standing, so I decided to visit them straight through their front door. In disguise, of course.

I had changed my hair, eye, and skin color, and had the jewelry I had worn when I attended Achille's party some time ago. The jewelry would draw attention away from the rest of my appearance, and it would make it harder for them to recognize me without the ornaments, just like a girl without the glasses she always wore.

...*I'm so smart!*

Plus, by wearing expensive jewelry, I could signify that I wasn't wanting for money, and make them less likely to suspect me of being a swindler attempting a desperate gamble to rip off some rich nobles. It helped give me some authority, too.

And to top it all off, I had my 'suspicious mask.' ...This ruined my authority and credibility all at once.

"So, you're the so-called potion maker from another land. Well? Do you mean to tell me that you have the Longevity Medicine?"

"No, why would I?"

The baron and the guard standing by near me wore the same shocked expression. Oh, and the guard was positioning himself so he could seize me right away if I made any suspicious movements.

Even if they were a lower-class baronial house, one removed from any intense political strife and not the type to attract grudges... Even then, being the head of a baronial house, he could never be completely safe from resentment or unwanted attention.

Therefore, they would obviously want to avoid any unnecessary danger. I may have looked powerless, but I could still be hiding weapons or poison. I even called myself a potion maker, so they *should* assume that I could handle poison as well.

"I do not handle medicines of *that* sort. My potions are much more effective."

"Wh-What?! More effective than the Longevity Medicine? It can't be... Well, I have heard of such things in distant lands, but they

say they are quick to spoil and hard to transport over long distances…
I've also heard this medicine hasn't been made for quite some time,
ever since the original creator passed away and its recipe was lost…"

Huh, this place was quite distant from the Kingdom of Balmore,
and I didn't think they would know about it, but he seemed to have
pretty accurate information about my potions. This information
should have been limited to the higher-ups, so a lowly baron
shouldn't even know about it…

Well, babbling on with explanations was a waste of time. And
if he didn't want to believe me, I didn't have to force him to take my
potions. If he refused my help, I would just take my leave. Francette
might end up a little disappointed, but that couldn't be helped.

There was no need to force my medicine on them, and as they
say, "Those who believe shall be saved," so I didn't intend to go out of
my way to take care of non-believers.

So…

fwsh

I gestured as if I was reaching into my pocket and pulled out a
single bottle.

"Here's the healing medicine, the Tears of the Goddess."

This wasn't the potion being sold to the masses in Balmore,
but the specially-made Tears of the Goddess delivered by the Angel
herself.

After all, I wasn't Shop Owner Kaoru right now, but rather the
'Angel.'

"Huh?" The baron and guard blurted out as they stared at me,
wide-eyed.

"Wha…"

Baron Dorivell was completely speechless.

"As I said, this is the healing medicine known as the Tears of the Goddess. If you have no need for it, I'll be taking it home… Oh, and it doesn't keep well, so it will be useless unless it's taken now."

The baron hesitated for just a moment.

"…Right this way!"

The baron led me into a child's room. A boy of about ten lay sick in his bed.

"Challotte, I brought you some new medicine! Drink!"

Baron Dorivell accepted the potion from me and handed it to his son. His hand was trembling slightly, but he focused on not spilling a single drop with a look of desperation. Though, honestly, spilling a little wouldn't really have affected the results. It seemed the boy wasn't actually asleep, and sat up to drink down the contents of the bottle his father held to his mouth.

Thinking about it, I did question how this noble was having his son drink medicine some strange girl had given him straight away. It would have been one thing in Balmore, where the angel and her deeds were well known, but… He must really have been out of options, or maybe he was just planning on punishing me after the fact if I had been lying. Well, maybe he figured not even a child would be dumb enough to pull off a stunt like that. Considering he had heard about the Tears of the Goddess, he must have been well aware of its instantaneous effects, too.

"Father, I feel better…"

"Y-You do?! Your fever—How about your fever?"

He clearly wanted to cry out in jubilation. But, afraid of being let down, he was using all his willpower to control his emotions. His face cycled rapidly between expressions, the baron still unable to believe in the miracle.

"The haziness and fever seem to be gone…"

The baron pressed a hand against his son's head, peered into his eyes, checked his tongue, and eventually seemed to understand that the illness truly had been cured. Maybe it wasn't some incurable, malignant disease... Well, by the standards of modern Japan, anyway.

But even an illness that could be cured in Japan, probably with a single shot or even just a better diet, could easily kill people in a lower-level civilization like this one. Especially younger children.

So, ultimately, I didn't know what sort of illness this boy had, or whether it would have been resolved through natural means, had he been left alone. But to this baronial house, I was definitely considered the Angel of the Goddess, the one who had saved their son's life.

This realization seemed to hit the baron suddenly, and he turned toward me and kneeled. Of course, this wasn't something a noble would do for an ordinary potion maker.

It was probably much easier to believe that I was the angel of the goddess, rather than thinking I was some potion-making 12-year-old genius who happened to have a miracle medicine with an extremely short shelf life, handing it over without even negotiating a price.

That is, according to the frame of reference possessed by this baron and his world... Yeah, I thought so, too.

"Lady Angel, I thank you from the bottom of my heart for saving my son, Challotte..."

Huh, he went straight to deciding I was the angel without any sort of confirmation? Don't tell me...

"You know of me?"

"Yes, I learned of your existence while researching various medicines for my son. The miracle medicine, known as the 'potion,' was said to have circulated in and around the Kingdom of Balmore for several years. They say a scary-look...children cri...girl with sharp eyes...was heavily involved in the creation and distribution of said potions. Then there were rumors of a girl with terrify... I mean, *intense* eyes, who was said to have stood in the shadows during the defeat and miraculous resurgence of the Aligot Empire four years ago, along with the fall of the Holy Land of Rueda and the glorious appearance of the Goddess Celestine. Also, there were the hidden workings of the secret organization, the Eyes of the Goddess, and the angel's salvation for the pure of heart... With our country being so far away, only the upper echelons seem to have grasped the full story, but even a lower-class noble of little means like myself can obtain such information, when possessed of desperate determination to save my child..."

...Okay, I get it! You don't have to put in so much effort to avoid saying my eyes are scary!

It makes me feel worse when you have to try so hard to be considerate about it!

...Damn it.

Well then, my job was done.

Time to go!

"Well, I've done what I came here to do, so I'll be excusing myself now..."

"Please wait! It would sully my honor if you were to leave without me repaying you! I beg of you, allow me to express my gratitude somehow!" the baron pleaded desperately.

Well, I suppose that was to be expected. I'm sure he didn't want to part ways forever after this one meeting, but it seemed he truly did want to thank me, so I decided to accept the usual: a small gift that he could manage without putting a strain on himself. I also had to make sure he kept quiet about this.

"First, I want you to promise you will never tell another soul about me. I don't want to deal with rude people with empty hearts, and I am not a fan of laying waste to entire countries... Though, really, it doesn't seem to bother Celes."

"Y-Y-Yes, of course! I swear by the Goddess herself!"

Wow, he actually seems terrified...

But I guess that was to be expected. There were many myths and legends of Celes destroying whole nations. In fact, the tale of how she left a scar on this very land was actually a true story.

"And, hmm... Well then, I'll accept some information as a token of your gratitude."

"...Information?" The baron looked at me with a blank expression. I mean, he was probably wondering what sort of information the angel could possibly want.

"Do you know of any royalty in this country who suffer from a serious illness or injury?"

He seemed to understand why I was asking the question.

"N-No, not in the royal families, or among the ducal families, for that matter. Though, if they were keeping such news private, I would naturally not be aware of it..."

Yeah, he was just a baron after all. He wouldn't know about the private affairs of the higher-ups unless he was investigating specific families. He must have spent a lot of money and effort to get information about the angel and potions, too.

"What about the noble houses of marquisate rank and lower?"

"Yes, there are several. Elderly heads of house, who have already passed their titles to their heirs; sick and feeble children; those who were injured while on horseback or in conflicts with other fiefs; those with lung diseases and other illnesses... When you include lower-class nobles, life peers, and their dependents, it adds up to quite a lot of people."

I thought so…

"So, what would you do if those people demanded that you tell them how your son was cured, or insisted that you introduce them to the potion maker who helped you?"

Yes, this was what I was really worried about.

The baron likely would have kept my secret if left unmolested, but I would have felt bad if he suffered for it.

"Oh, you needn't worry about that… That I've been searching far and wide for medicine, for skilled apothecaries, and have consequently gotten involved with charlatans, is quite well known. So, if I say one of them healed my son, no one could be certain which of them happened to have succeeded, and no one would expect me to know where some vagrant potion maker might be. And, just in case…"

With that, the baron looked me in the eye and spoke with a serious expression.

"Please tell me the following: 'If anyone asks about me and tries to force you to speak, I will first kill them and their entire family. I will only speak to them afterward.' There would be no need to actually carry this out, of course. The purpose is so I can say that this is what I've been told."

The heck is that?! How are they supposed to speak to me after I killed them?

Besides, their injured and sick would be dead by that point, so there would be no need for the Angel or the Tears of the Goddess!

Though, that would resolve the issue…

"Please do not worry. I won't ever reveal anything, so there will never be any need for you to spill blood in this particular instance."

… 'In *this* particular instance'? He made it sound like I'd been slaughtering people left and right! Come on, now... Did he assume I was like Celes because of her particular history? I wasn't the type to decimate entire countries just because I got a little fed up! ...Wait, had I done that once? No, no, I only flipped over a nation's entire structure. It wasn't as if I massacred its people and destroyed the entire land.

I'm not like Celes, I swear!

Well, whatever. Don't fret over the small stuff!

"All right, then. Here it goes. 'If anyone asks about me and tries to force you to speak, I will first kill them and their entire family. I will only speak to them afterward.' Good?"

"Yes, thank you!"

All right, my job here is done.

"Well then, I'll be…"

"Please wait!"

Again?!

"I ask that you at least accept this as thanks!"

With that, he held out a small, weighty-looking leather bag.

It looked just like one of those bags of gold you see people hand out as they say, 'Here's your reward!' ...Wait, that's exactly what it was!

When did he even have a chance to get that ready? ...Hey, there's a butler-looking guy standing behind the baron! Where'd he come from?!

But he was a lower-class noble, and must have spent quite a lot of money looking for a cure for his son... He was probably using up all his available funds and grasping at straws for rumors that weren't all that believable, or treatments that probably wouldn't work, hoping against hope... I would have felt bad for putting more financial strain on him. It wasn't as if I was wanting for money, anyway.

"No, I don't accept those types of payments. I only take small tokens of... Oh, I know!"

With that, I took the leather pouch and loosened the strap that held it closed. Then I dumped out its contents onto the table.

Ahh, this hand-feel! It was the 'leather bag for gold coins' reward that I've always wanted!

"I'll be taking this!"

"Huh? Wh-What...?"

The baron was dumbfounded. But I didn't care!

This texture is absolutely amazing! Could it be buckskin? *Or leather from some slain monster, to keep the cost low?*

In any case, this was quite enough for my 'token of gratitude.' I was way happier with this than I would have been with some Chanel bag! Yes, I know, I could have just asked someone where to buy a bag like this. But I wanted something to remember this meeting by. Though, to be honest, I couldn't really think of anything else to accept as thanks.

I decided to provide a follow-up explanation.

"The coins in the bag were full of the love and care that the parents and servants of this house have for this child, and full of gratitude for the Goddess. This bag is brimming with the love that has been imbued into it by the coins... Are you familiar with a dish known as simmered beril and daikon?"

"Y-Yes, I've had it before..."

Beril was a fish that was a lot like buri... In fact, it could have been the same exact fish. I couldn't tell the minute differences apart, but when I ate it, it seemed like the same fish. And daikon was, well, Japanese radish.

With my automatic translation ability, the fish came up in my mind as "beril," and the plant came up as "daikon," though it could have been that it was something else entirely, but I didn't know the distinction.

What was the difference?!

...Anyway, "simmered beril and daikon" was basically simmered buri and daikon. Even though he was a lower-class noble, I was a bit surprised that the baron had eaten this dish before. It was totally considered 'commoner food.' Well, it meant there wasn't any need for explanations, so that was fine by me.

"Then I'm certain you will understand. With that dish, the beril seems to be the main component, but that's not the case. The daikon, which has absorbed the beril's umami, is the star of the show! The beril is nothing more than a component. Likewise, the Goddess will appreciate this leather bag that has soaked up your love and faith, far more than she would have the gold that has given it up already. Now, if you'll excuse me, I will take my leave."

There, a perfect follow-up. I'd successfully evaded the baron's gift of coins without making him look bad.

This time, I can finally retreat in good order!

At the baron's house, after Kaoru had left...

"I see... The pouch that has absorbed our thoughts and feelings has far greater worth than the gold coins... Are you kidding me?!" the baron shouted out loudly.

"Indeed..." his butler replied, with an awkward smile, "That must have been..."

"Yes. A ruse on the Angel's part, out of consideration for our financial situation. An incredibly obvious one, at that... She may be good at performing miracles, but she's completely lacking in acting ability. With her s-strange mask..."

Then he stood from his seat and went down on his knees again to pray, sobbing all the while, while the butler left the room in silence.

*   *

When I returned from the baron's place, my guards were waiting for me. This time, it was the full cast of fighters: Francette, Roland, and Emile. I'd never consider Belle a fighter, since she'd die trying to take one enemy down with her. And so, Belle stayed behind to watch the shop with Layette.

The others stayed away from me, of course. They would have ruined the whole point of my disguise if they had been hovering around me. It would have been a dead giveaway, so they had to keep some distance between us and act like strangers, at least until I found some secluded place to remove my disguise.

They had been waiting outside, just in case something went wrong at the baron's house, but I doubt there were many in this world who would dare try something with me. And by 'try something,' I mean to try taking advantage of me, knowing that I am the angel. That would be one easy way to incur Celes' wrath. Celes was pretty quick to anger, and had no reservations about killing humans. The people of this world were well aware of this.

There were several well-known examples in the recent past, and there was a painful reminder left over in the form of a scar on the continent.

Yeah, no. No thanks to using that sort of force.

Anyway, it was time for me to go home and prepare dinner.

* *

I closed down the shop for the day to go out with everyone. The destination? A pasture in the suburbs. It was about time I went to pay a visit, or they were going to get upset again. By "they," I mean Ed and the others.

So, the six of us went to practice horseback riding.

"Ed, we're here!"

"Ohh, you're here!"

"Welcome."

"Got any sugar cubes, Big Sis Kaoru?"

Ed's family seemed to be the same as ever.

"How's life here?"

"The food is great here, thanks to you paying extra, and we can roam the riding grounds and grass fields freely, and I can always be with my family, so I'm more than happy! I love the looks of envy the others have been giving me, too!"

"Ahaha…"

Roland and Francette were bonding with their own horses next to us. Oh, and they were also getting fed the special food, like corn, carrots, apples, and sugar cubes, of course. I had given the sugar cubes to the manager myself.

…He may have been taking a cut for himself, but I was willing to let it slide a little. As long as it was just for his family and he wasn't reselling them, that is.

Roland and Francette were apparently the type to really care for their horses, brushing and providing a lot of physical contact and affection. They were well cared for, thanks to the additional fees I'd been paying, but this was something else altogether.

The horses were saying, "Not like that! Brush along the hairs with more gentleness and love!" but I decided not to tell them.

Emile and Belle rode Ed's wife and daughter to lightly trot around the area, while I had Layette ride Ed. Ed's daughter may have been smaller and easier to ride than Ed, but I had more experience with riding Ed, so I felt more confident in trusting him with Layette.

You never knew what kind of unexpected mistake could occur with the combination of an inexperienced rider and a horse, so I wouldn't have felt at ease otherwise.

I told Ed as such, and he said, "That's right, you totally get it," with a satisfied expression.

We usually traveled by chariot, but there were times when we rode together with Layette in my arms, and she might have to ride by herself in an emergency some time.

I explained this to Ed and Layette, and told them to master how to ride fast while prioritizing their safety. And with me translating Ed's comments to Layette, Layette quickly improved her riding skills, just like I had.

Afterwards, I had Belle and Layette train to escape with the two of them riding one horse. This was in preparation for a potential scenario in which I was buying time with Ed while Belle helped Layette escape. They protested that they would never run away without me, but when I insisted that it was an order, they reluctantly did as they were told.

Though, in this scenario, I'd actually be making them retreat not so I could buy some time, but because I wouldn't want them to see how terribly I'd end up devastating the opponent.

"...Well? What is it, Ed?"

"Huh...?"

"There's something you want to discuss or ask of me, isn't there? I know you, Ed. I can tell. There's no need for modesty between us. Just spit it out while we're alone over here. Though... it would just sound like neighing to them, even if they were in earshot."

"Guess nothing gets past you..."

After hesitating for a moment, Ed opened his mouth.

"Thing is, there's a good-natured old guy here at this pasture. He's really nice, telling me all sorts of funny stories and keeping my daughter entertained with his chats. But one day, he fell asleep while laying out in the sun. He said in his sleep... 'This is revenge for my master!' 'Miss, that's the murderer!' I realized there were tears running down his face..."

Hmm, maybe this old man's a caretaker for the horses? Someone with a complicated past...

"Unlike humans, we horses don't shed tears often. Only for something real serious."

...Wait, this "old guy" was a horse?!

Oh, he did mention that they were talking to each other. Of course it was a horse.

"This old guy's going to be put down soon. He can't pull carriages, carry riders, or be a workhorse at the farm anymore. But still... Still. I want to do something for him! When he goes, I want him to go with a smile, satisfied with the life he lived!"

"Ed... have you realized?"

"Huh? Realized what?"

"You're shedding tears right now..."

If Ed felt so strongly about it, I couldn't stand by and do nothing. After all, Ed was my beloved horse, friend... and brother in arms.

All right, I'll do it!

"My mount and sacred horse, Ed, I will grant your wish. Stand by my side and strike down the immoral!"

"It would be my honor..."

"We will help as well, Ed!" Roland and Francette's horses neighed.

Were they trying to get on my good side because I'm a goddess? Or maybe they wanted Ed's favor because they're into his daughter...

Oh, well. The greater the numbers, the better.

This was a request from my own horse, so I couldn't involve Francette, Roland, Emile, or Belle. I was doing this for my own reasons, so I didn't want to drag unrelated people into it. But these two horses had offered to help the old horse of their own accord, so I didn't mind accepting their assistance.

It wasn't as if they'd need to do anything, so they'd be out of harm's way, anyhow. They'd simply be accomplices in this.

So…

"Okay. Everyone, we need to keep this a secret from Roland, Francette, and the others, so laugh together with me to avoid suspicion. Ready? Aaand…"

"Breeehehehe!" neighed the horses, completely naturally.

"Ahahaha!"

If you suddenly saw your horse walk over to me, exchange some words, then start laughing in an exaggerated way…

Yeah, you'd probably have that look on your face. That dubious, judging expression…

When Roland and Francette asked me what our conversation had been about, I told them that my jokes even land on horses, but it was a pun that only worked in their language, so humans wouldn't understand.

Ed pointed out the old horse in question, and I told the others I was going to check in with the other horses to make sure Ed had been behaving.

"Are you Carlos?"

"Wha—?! A talking human? Impossible!"

…

……

I suppose that was the expected reaction…

Oh, well. I'm not really a human, anyway. All right, mode change time!

"I am a friend of Celestine, the goddess of this world. You are Carlos, I presume?"

"L-Lady Goddess! I am not worthy!"

The old horse, Carlos, lowered his head in a hurry.

"I have given my sacred horse, Ed, time to rest and spend time with his family in this world, but he has brought me here to fulfill a personal request. He claims you have been good to him, and asks that I grant your wish... So, as a reward for his hard work, I have decided to grant him his request. Now, what is it you desire?"

Yeah, I'll go with this setting this time. This should get him to speak openly.

...But were these really horses I was dealing with?

Do horses really have a language that allows them to communicate so comprehensively? Just with a combination of neighs and snorts? They say horses are less intelligent than dogs, and dogs are supposedly as smart as three-year-old humans, putting them lower than cats, but above rabbits, in the intelligence tier list.

Though, I'm sure there are differences between each individual, and it varies by type of intelligence... like numbers, pattern recognition, memory, and comprehension... making it hard to make a sweeping generalization, but...

It was still strange that we could have such advanced communication like this. Celes must have...

No, no, don't think about it! This is just how it is! Don't dig too deep into it! Just let the small details slide. In fact, don't worry about the big details, either.

It was a bit late to start thinking about this, after I had talked with Ed and the others so often.

"Now, tell me. What is your wish...?"

"M-My wish... Th-That is..."

"Yes?"

"The young mistress! My wish is to save her!"

Thought so...

Then, Carlos began explaining.

He was once a riding horse who belonged to a certain noble family. When he was five years old, the noble husband and wife had another child after having their firstborn son.

Ten years later, Carlos was given to this daughter, due to his gentle nature and many years of experience as a riding horse.

Being late in his years, the parents must have figured Carlos wouldn't run around recklessly. Fifteen years was quite old for a horse, after all. He wasn't a stud suitable for breeding, and since he didn't have any offspring of his own, Carlos saw this ten-year-old human girl like he would his own child or granddaughter.

He spent his days peacefully, fulfilling his role as this noble girl's riding horse, which was likely to be the last duty given to him.

These quiet days continued, as he thought they would until he met his eventual end. That's what he thought, anyway.

Until, one day…

When the girl was fourteen years old and Carlos was nineteen, the carriage the family was riding in was attacked. Her parents and brother all lost their lives, leaving only the girl, who had stayed at home.

Her grandparents were already deceased, making the girl the sole survivor, with no close family to care for her. Then, her father's younger brother—in other words, her uncle—came into her house, claimed that his older brother had told him to take care of the girl if something ever happened to him, and demanded her hand in marriage.

The girl said she would do what her father had wanted and thus obeyed. But one day, when the girl and her uncle passed by the stable, two carriage horses said in surprise:

"That's the guy who was ordering the attackers around…"

Carlos heard as much clearly with his own ears. The girl had explained the details to him after her family had passed away. She had always told him everything, though she was mostly speaking to herself. She didn't care whether her horse understood her or not.

"Say, Carlos. I don't like my uncle very much, but if it's my father's wish, I will marry him and protect this house. Stay by my side, okay, Carlos? Don't ever leave me…"

He still remembered the words she had said to him while stroking his hair.

This was a difficult request for a horse, which has a shorter life expectancy than a human, and this was an aged horse, at that. But Carlos wanted to do what he could to make her wish come true. Carlos felt the blood rising to his head. Something burned within him, like all the blood in his entire body was boiling over.

And in contrast, there was a heavy, cold lump deep inside him.

Anger.

Hate.

And again, anger.

When the uncle went to the stable by himself to go out one day, Carlos tried and failed to kick him to death, and unfamiliar humans had taken him away and brought him out here the next day.

He figured the people here were allowing him to live out his final days in peace, out of simple kindness. His life would soon come to an end, and he would depart from this world.

But if there was such a thing as souls and the afterlife… If it was possible to curse a man to death with sheer anger and hate… If such a thing as demons existed in this world…

…I shall become the devil himself, and drag him straight to hell!

Heavy. That was… very heavy. But all I could say was one thing:

"Very well, leave it to me. You shall have your revenge…"

Oh, no. This makes me sound more like a malevolent god than a goddess.

I left Carlos behind as he dexterously bent his legs to prostrate himself, and joined the others.

Then, I reported what had happened to Ed and the horse crew. This was all in horse language, so Francette and the others obviously didn't understand what I said.

For my report, I told them…

"Vengeance is mine."

This wasn't a reference to the title of a famous movie. It actually originated from a passage in the New Testament, which essentially meant, "Humans aren't the ones who bring retribution to humans. It is my role as God."

"Okay, everyone, laugh!"

If they were to lower their heads or act meekly here, Francette or Emile might not have noticed anything, but Roland was pretty sharp, so he may have found it suspicious. So, just like earlier, I wanted to make them think I had cracked another joke.

"Breeehehehe!!!" I laughed along with the three horses, excluding Ed's wife and child.

Roland and Francette gave me a look, but I totally ignored them.

Afterwards, I had the others continue bonding with their horses, and I headed toward the caretaker's office. I told them I was going to discuss the horses' care and settle payments, so no one tried to follow me. There was no perceived threat here, and everyone wanted to cherish their time with their horses, so this was to be expected.

That was exactly why I had used an unexciting reason for leaving anyway.

"Please sell me that old horse named Carlos!"

I didn't know when Carlos would finally be put down if I didn't do something about it. I decided it would be best for me to buy him, just in case. A nineteen-year-old horse was about eighty in human years. He couldn't be too expensive.

"He's a mild-mannered and intelligent horse, but he's quite advanced in his years."

"I understand that. I intend for him to spend his days gently interacting with humans, rather than doing any physical labor… For the time he has left, that is…"

The old custodian's eyes widened a bit as if out of surprise, then he lowered his head.

"…Please, take good care of him."

He knew I was someone who didn't mind spending money on my horses, considering I was already paying a higher rate to ensure that Ed was well taken care of. And I was clearly a wealthy customer, seeing as how I was paying for the care of five horses by myself. Being polite to a good customer was just common sense.

But it seemed that wasn't all. Taking care of animals is hard work. Considering how he was still doing this all the way out in the outskirts at his age, he must have held a deep love for horses, or animals in general.

So, when an old horse that could no longer work, one that was just waiting to be put down, could live out its final days happily with a horse-loving, rich customer, there was no way he wouldn't be happy about that.

He must have had his guard down from that happiness right now. Now was my chance!

"How did Carlos end up here?"

"Oh, you see, he was a riding horse for a noble house for a long time, but once he became old, he tried to harm the new master of the house, and was sent here to be disposed of… But like the other horses of the Viscount Raphael's house, Carlos has been under my care for many years, and I simply cannot believe such a thing to be true! Carlos is smart, gentle, and loves people… But I could not refuse the orders his owner gave to dispose of him. So, I thought I could at least let him live out his final days in peace…"

He's tearing up. What a nice person…

Oh, but…

"If he ordered you to dispose of him, won't you get in trouble for selling him?"

To which he answered, "Ah, but his orders were, 'Dispose of this horse. The money you get for selling the meat should be enough payment for your trouble.' Which means that there is no issue with me selling Carlos and receiving payment for the meat. After all, as he said, I am 'disposing' of him and getting paid for the 'meat.' Whether that 'meat' is dead or alive is up to my personal discretion."

Wow, he's all smiles right now…

"But wouldn't it be bad for you if the viscount finds out?"

"…Is that an issue?"

He was more concerned about this old horse than displeasing the viscount's house! Maybe he empathized with Carlos, being in his later years himself? But I didn't mind dealing with people like that.

All right, leave it to me!

"…So, will you opt for the additional rates for Carlos as well?"

Oh, right, he'll be considered my horse now, too.

"Yes, please. I'd like his meals, brushing, and grazing conditions to be the same as the other five horses."

There, now I'd secured Carlos's safety. I'd even found out the name of his former owner. The nouns the horses used weren't much help to me, after all.

Yes, everything was going just as planned...

*   *

"...Even if it costs my life!" recited Emile and Belle together.

"Like I said, your lives are more important to me than a request from a horse I just met!"

No matter how many times I told them not to, these fools always tried to prioritize any little request from me over their own lives. That's why I had to be extremely cautious about any order or request I gave them...

"How many times do I have to say this?! It would be a huge loss for me if any of you were to die! Can you really call yourselves loyal if you're willing to just throw away two of my subjects?"

"Urgh..." they groaned, dejectedly.

I've been through this routine so many times. When are they going to learn...?

I'd learned that it was impossible for a complete amateur like me to covertly gather intel. As such, I had no choice but to enlist Emile and Belle, and just let the specialists do their work. Leave rice cakes to the rice cake shop, as they say.

Emile and Belle were members of the Eyes of the Goddess, an organization that supported those of my activities that bring salvation to the good of heart. You could say that this specific task would bring salvation to these two in particular, who had been feeling down from me not giving them any work, so whatever.

Francette and Roland could start saying this or that if they found out, and I didn't want to drag them into my personal matters or things involving the nobility and their betrothed, so I decided to keep them out of it. I had to make sure they didn't find out…

Layette? Well, she was always with me, so… Haha…

"Anyway, my first order is, 'No dying.'"

"My second order is, 'I'll allow some degree of injury, but you are to avoid getting seriously hurt by any means necessary.'"

"My third order is, 'Maintain secrecy.'"

"And the fourth is, 'Gather information.'"

"Don't overextend yourselves. If you sense even a little danger, you must retreat immediately and report what you've found up to that point. If you're caught, or if it seems like you can't escape, declare that you're a servant of the Goddess and bring whoever caught you to me. That way, I can get you back, along with the information you've obtained, and the enemy will be in my court. If you resist and end up getting killed, I'll lose all of that. Which outcome do you think would be more beneficial to me?"

"…Us coming back alive…" said the two, in a dull monotone.

There, that should be enough to prevent them from doing anything stupid. It always takes so much effort to deal with them…

"Okay then, focus on the main objectives. I'll leave the rest to you two."

I sent Emile and Belle out to gather intel, and now all I had to do was wait.

Oh, but it wasn't like they were going to infiltrate a noble's manor or anything like that. That would've been a quick way to get them killed.

Their specialty was acting like bystanders who just happened to be present, listening in on conversations, and manipulating conversations as if just making small talk, in order to get the information they wanted. Before, they also used that they were children as a tool for deceiving people, but Emile didn't have that option now that he was an adult.

Belle, on the other hand, could apparently still pull it off...

I wondered if she looked up at people with her puppy-dog eyes and said something like, "Please, mister!" If I tried that, they'd probably think I was picking a fight, and I'd end up making them angry...

*   *

"...So, that horse, Carlos, was handed over to the pasture about two months ago to be disposed of. It was right after the viscount's family carriage was attacked by bandits, and the uncle began staying at their house. The viscount's daughter will turn fifteen, making her an adult, in four months. We still have time."

I didn't think Carlos had much time left, so I was right in assuming that it hadn't been very long since the incident. I was relieved.

The daughter not being of age yet was fortunate, too. Since she wasn't married due to age rather than a refusal, the uncle probably wouldn't try to force her into marriage before she turned fifteen. He only had to wait a little longer to get married officially, so it was unlikely that he would do something to cause problems or make her hate him. The people of this world were pretty accepting of that sort of thing, but royalty and titled nobility really valued lineage, so they cared about having a "pure" bride...

This didn't really apply to mistresses, but when it came to a lawful wife whose child could become the heir, she was expected to be completely celibate... Though I guess that goes without saying. In

118

any case, we still had four months until the daughter's marriage, so we'd be fine until then.

You could even fix a jet plane in four whole months!

"And they have two riding horses, four carriage horses, and two carriages. It seems they've had all of the horses for over two years. In addition, they have three guard dogs, which are also used for hunting foxes. The daughter, who loves animals, has been helping with their care."

All right, let's start from there.

*   *

"An animal doctor?"

"Indeed, with the teachings that have been passed down through our family line, I am able to check your animals for any issues of the mind and body, and thus resolve them."

A suspicious individual had visited the house of Viscount Raphael. Pale skin, chestnut hair, and kindly, drooping blue eyes.

This was, of course, Kaoru.

She had changed the color of her skin, hair, and eyes with a potion, and used adhesive and exceptional makeup skills to force her eyes, which were normally turned up at the corners, to droop down instead.

Kaoru was a 22-year-old working adult in her previous life, so she did know how to use makeup. She preferred not to cake the makeup on, opting instead for a natural look, but she was capable of transforming herself to a degree that could be considered trickery, if she wanted. Especially now that she had things like "cosmetics-type potions that fix skin blemishes"…

Hair and skin colors were one thing, but with the change in her eye shape, no one would ever see this girl and know it was Kaoru.

Kaoru revised!

...Which wasn't too surprising, considering her entire raison d'être had been changed.

"You look suspicious... Well, just wait here for now. You might end up entertaining the mistress, so I'll at least announce you. But if this ends up being some sort of scam, you'll get what's coming to you..."

With that, one of the guards disappeared into the manor. The other stayed to keep an eye on this suspicious girl.

"Well then, I'll start checking for issues now."

"You'd better not be planning on saying nothing was wrong, then charging us anyway," the young retainer responded mockingly to Kaoru's comment.

...I say 'young,' but he was probably in his late twenties or early thirties.

Other than Kaoru and this retainer, an old man on stable duty, an aging man who seemed to be a butler, and the daughter of Viscount Raphael—rather, the present head of House Raphael, Mariel—were in the stable, bringing the total to five people. The uncle in question wasn't present.

120

All right, just as planned! It's only been about two months since she lost her family. She should still be burdened with sorrow and confusion from the loss, so her retainers won't miss this chance to cheer her up, considering her love for animals. I knew I wouldn't be turned away at the gates!

Of course, even if she had been, she would have just come up with another plan.

This is why Kaoru had gone in with an optimistic attitude, and ended up being surprised that her first attempt had actually worked out.

"...Now, let us begin."

Kaoru ignored the retainer's words, facing the six horses with a serious expression.

"I am Kaoru. I have come here to fulfill the wish of my devout servant, Carlos. Which of you wishes to avenge your master?"

"Whaaaaaaaaaat?!" the six horses shouted in surprise.

"C-Carlos... Even in death, you think of our young mistress... A-Aaaaaaahhh!"

"I couldn't do anything, despite still being alive... I'm so ashamed..."

Tears fell from the eyes of the horses.

"We would do anything for our master and the young miss!"

"We, too, swear loyalty and shall become sacred horses as Carlos did!"

"Uoooooohhh!" the horses wailed together.

"Oh, Carlos is still alive."

"Whaaaaaaaaaat?!" they yelled, their wailing stopping abruptly.

The household of Viscount Raphael simply watched the horses getting riled up, entirely dumbfounded...

Chapter 33:
Road to Revenge

Something was clearly off.

The mysterious girl and horses continued to neigh and whinny back and forth. The only possible explanation was that they were communicating somehow, and the horses were reacting extremely strangely as a result.

The members of the viscount's household remained frozen in confusion, but the current head of the house, Mariel, was the only one motionless due to an emotion other than surprise.

Ahh, if only I had met this girl sooner! Maybe I could have talked to Carlos before he died...

Apparently, Mariel had been told that Carlos had died suddenly and unexpectedly.

Kaoru's conversation with the horses continued, regardless of what was going through the minds of the others.

"Oh, I came in here claiming to be a veterinarian. I need to do something to make it look believable. Do any of you have any injuries or illnesses? I'll make you all better. If you have anything you want to tell these humans, I can relay those messages too."

"Really?!" the horses said.

Then, they conversed for a while in neighs and whinnies.

"This horse says, 'A horrible man whipped me needlessly just to work out his frustration. My butt still hurts.' Did someone lend this horse to a piece of trash who abuses animals?"

"Wha…" the humans replied, stunned.

The only person I could think of was that uncle in question.

"And this other riding horse says, 'My knee hurts because the man who sold Carlos to a stable to dispose of him rides very aggressively.'"

"Ah!" said Mariel, having been rendered nearly speechless by the first half of Kaoru's comment.

"Oh…" the butler and old stable keeper said quietly. They had frozen up, as the truth they had decided to keep secret from the young mistress had just been revealed.

But the bombs didn't end there. If that had been a 50-kilo bomb, the next one would be an atom bomb.

"And this carriage horse seems to be experiencing some mental anguish. 'I hate that I have to let the killer of my master and his family ride me. The young mistress is being deceived. I don't want her riding with him…'"

"Whaaaaaat!!!" they all yelled out.

They were shocked. Dazed.

"Wh-Wha… What do you mean…?"

"I mean, that's what the horse is saying. I don't know anything about it. You should also be aware of their other concerns…"

Mariel was trembling, all the color drained from her face. The butler should have been supporting her, for fear of her falling over, but he was too preoccupied with his own worries.

"The carriage leans to the left due to a faulty wheel, which makes it hard for the horses to run. This one's saddle has a thorn in it, so he wants you to take it out. They also want apples and corn in their food every day, and sweets every once in a while."

Each of the things Kaoru pointed out were confirmed to be accurate by the stable keeper. A wound that seemed to be caused by a whip on a horse's rear. A horse that had been favoring its left leg to keep pressure off the right. A splinter stuck in a saddle. The left wheel of the carriage wasn't turning smoothly...

Did that mean the girl was right about the other things, as well? Could the horses really have told her such things, and could they be true?

"..."

The silence, which had only lasted a dozen seconds, felt like an eternity. A never-ending, dragging silence...

Mariel seemed to finally reboot afterward, and asked Kaoru to translate for the horses. It was obvious what she wanted to ask about...

"...Is what they said," Kaoru finished interpreting for the horses.

Previously, they had conducted various experiments, such as blocking Kaoru's view of the horses by standing between them and making her turn the other way while keeping an eye on her, then having Kaoru order them to do complex movements and to neigh a specific number of times.

They also asked her things that only the stable keeper would know. Her credibility was proven without a shadow of a doubt. Silence filled the room again. They knew who the culprit was, but there was nothing they could do...

They could publicly accuse him, but the only proof they had was the word of some strange girl saying that the horses told her so. No one would take that seriously. The others had only heard horse noises, so this suspicious girl could just say whatever she wanted. And even if the horses could testify in the human tongue, they belonged to the person making the accusation, so they wouldn't be credible witnesses.

They needed something concrete that would be considered usable evidence by everyone. It was impossible to match fingerprints or extract DNA from hair in this world; even if that technology did exist, it wouldn't help find the culprit in this case. After all, the general population and those who conducted the trial wouldn't understand their significance.

"What should we do...?"

Mariel's question wasn't the query of someone who was actually at a loss for what to do. There was really only one thing to do; the question was how she could accomplish it for certain. Mariel didn't mean to ask what they should do about this situation, as such, but how to make it a reality. This was evident by the look in her eyes.

She intends to do whatever it takes...

It originally seemed that she had gotten married to her uncle as part of simply going with the flow, without ever thinking for herself, but that didn't seem to be the case. It turned out that she thought it was what her parents wanted. That must be why she had agreed to a marriage she didn't even want.

But if that was a lie, and her parents had never truly wanted such a thing... And if the very man who had tricked her was responsible for the death of her parents and brother...

Kaoru had considered withdrawing from this whole ordeal if Mariel was hesitant to do anything about it. She could create a potion that would make everyone involved forget about everything that had transpired in the last few minutes. The girl could marry her family's killer and live a modestly happy life.

Surely, she wouldn't mind such a fate. Ignorance is bliss, after all.

Carlos would be taken care of for the remainder of his life, at least so long as that old man was paid. Assuming the old man didn't die first, that is. That said, Carlos was quite old himself, and it was far more likely for a horse, which has a shorter life span than a human, to pass away first.

But this girl was prepared to take action. There was no sign of hesitation. And so, Kaoru knew what she must tell her.

"I actually do other work besides being an animal doctor."

This line was completely out of place in this heavy atmosphere. Which meant there must be something to it. Mariel gulped, waiting for Kaoru's next words.

Then, Kaoru spoke.

"To strike down unforgivable evil, and help the powerless achieve vengeance. They call me the Divine Punisher of Annihilation!"

Mariel and the others stood dumbfounded, then the girl remembered Kaoru's words from earlier.

"I actually do other work besides being an animal doctor."

Work. If this is her job...

"Please, fulfill my... no, House Raphael's request!"

The butler and the old stable keeper didn't seem surprised by Mariel's words, nor did they try to stop her. This was to be expected. That's what their calm demeanor seemed to convey. But in their eyes, there burned a flame of hatred.

Kaoru's reply was obvious:

"I refuse."

"Whaaaaaat?!"

A flat-out refusal. This was completely unexpected, considering how the conversation was going. The three from House Raphael stood agape, and Kaoru went on.

"I don't do double contracts."

Confused, Mariel gave her a blank expression, and Kaoru continued.

"I've already taken on a request from Carlos."

Mariel's eyes widened, then she shouted out loud.

"Oh Carlos! You care for me even in death!"

"Ahh... Carlos..."

"What a loyal horse he was..."

The stable keeper and butler crumpled in tears next to Mariel.

"Oh, uh, Carlos isn't dead... But no one's listening..."

*　　　*

"What? Carlos is alive?"

"At least when I received his request, yeah. It seemed like he had a few years in him before he died of old age," I explained to Mariel von Raphael.

Though, it was possible that the old horse could have died an hour ago without me knowing, so I didn't make an irresponsible remark like, "He's alive right now." You just never know when it comes to the elderly. But I had given him a potion, just in case, so I doubted that would be an issue.

And so, the investigation was done, and now it was time for the revenge stage.

"I will be fulfilling Carlos's request now. Can I ask for your cooperation?"

Nod, nod.

It was time to execute the plan. I didn't intend to have the humans help directly. This was a request from Carlos, on behalf of his owner, the previous viscount, and this young girl. That was why Mariel, the current viscountess of House Raphael, didn't want to involve the others, either. The only ones who would be part of this were the ones who were in the same position and held the same feelings as Carlos.

"Please show me where you keep the dogs here."

*   *

"What... is that?"

"Creeps me out..."

The people regarded the residence with fear and loathing.

It didn't seem particularly out of the ordinary, though it was a bit more luxurious than the average commoner could afford, the kind of home that a modestly wealthy merchant or a noble without a title would live in. Yes, nothing out of the ordinary.

That is, if one disregarded the massive murder of crows atop the roof, trees, and walls, and the many dogs sitting around its perimeter...

"Damn it, just what is going on here?! Why are there so many crows and dogs all around this house? Did someone scatter food as a prank?"

Aragorn von Raphael... The younger brother of Mariel's father. In other words, the second son of the previous generation of House Raphael, and Mariel's uncle. Currently twenty-eight years old.

He was a bit far from Mariel's father in age, and Mariel was currently fourteen, having been born when her father was twenty, so her uncle was now exactly twice her age. When it came to marriage between nobles, a twenty-year difference in age was quite common, and a marriage between an uncle and his niece was not uncommon, particularly when the purpose of said marriage was to protect a family's inheritance.

A second son was only considered the "reserve" in matters of inheritance, and as soon as the first son and heir had a child, the second son's role as that reserve was greatly diminished. This was particularly true if the newborn was a boy, but it was also much the same for girls. In that case, the girl would simply be married off to a noble house's second son, or even lower, and there would be plenty of willing candidates.

Such a marriage would result in blood ties to that family, and such strategic marriages could be quite beneficial. So, if something did end up happening to the firstborn son, House Raphael would have arranged a strategic marriage for Mariel.

Mariel would have been able to choose one of the many candidates with good backgrounds, charming personalities, and fine appearances, and House Raphael would thus have gained a strong tie to a powerful noble's house. The son of the other house, who didn't have a future as the successor of the family title, would become the husband of the future head of household, and his family would eventually have their grandchild as the head of a noble house, so everything worked out in the end.

The firstborn son of House Raphael was clever and healthy, and Mariel was a beautiful and astute young girl. Whether they both grew up healthy, or if one of them happened to perish due to accident or illness, the future of House Raphael was stable. If everything had stayed as it was, everyone would have been happy.

That is, everyone other than Aragorn, who had no chance of inheriting the family title, and thus had no other choice but to become a military officer or a bureaucrat. And so, he had risked it all on one move: hiring assassins to murder his brother, his brother's wife, and his nephew.

Afterwards, he claimed that his brother had told him to take care of Mariel if anything happened to them, and so he demanded her hand in marriage. He figured his niece was an obedient child who loved and respected her parents, making her unlikely to resist his advances. Mariel would turn fifteen soon, making her an adult, and at that point they would get married, just as he had planned...

Making him the new head and viscount of House Raphael.

Normally, a man marrying into the family wouldn't inherit the family title, and he would simply be the "consort of the viscountess." This was to avoid a stranger with no blood ties ultimately inheriting the family title, in the case of divorce or remarriage after the wife passed away. But this time was different.

Aragorn himself had a right to inherit the family title, and if his brother's bloodline ended, the title would go to him. As such, there would be no inheritance issues if something were to happen to Mariel. His original plan was actually to wipe out the entire family, including Mariel. She ended up surviving due to her not being present at the time of the attack, but he was fine with that result.

Aragorn hated his brother for making him feel inferior and robbing him of the family title and fortune, and now he could make his brother's young and beautiful daughter serve him and do with her as he pleased. He was reveling in the sweet, sadistic joy that this thought brought him. If she refused, he would just have his assassins kill her, as he had the rest of her family. The title would still fall into his lap in the end.

With these thoughts in mind, Aragorn was completely unconcerned with the future. Such incidents occurring in a short time span would be problematic, but the "accident" would simply need to happen before Mariel married anyone else and had a child. And even if she did have a child, they would both just need to end up in an accident together. After all, whoever married her wouldn't have the right to inheritance if they weren't of Raphael blood.

But all of this planning soon became unnecessary, since Mariel had immediately agreed to the marriage. The first and second in line of House Raphael were to be married, and so the inheritance question was set aside. Just a few more months... Mariel would become fifteen in just a few more months, then...

His days had been spent in excitement with such thoughts, then this happened.

"What in the world... How ominous..."

With such a highly unusual thing recurring for multiple consecutive days, rumors had begun spreading, along with speculation.

"A house surrounded by a mass of crows and dogs."

"Maybe a witch or demon lives there."

"Someone who made a pact with a demon could be living there..."

From there, someone who had knowledge of the situation added to the rumors.

"I heard a noble husband and wife and their child were killed there."

"They say he's marrying the fourteen-year-old girl, who's the last survivor in line for the title..."

"Wait, don't tell me..."

"Who do you think those crows and dogs serve? The demon, or the husband and wife?"

Then, the house gradually became covered in the urine and feces of the crows and dogs. Not just from the crows and dogs in the area, but crows that flew in from other regions and dogs that walked over out of nowhere. They all left some droppings and went about their business. No one could deny the involvement of something supernatural after seeing such a sight. After all, this was a world where the existence of a goddess was an undeniable fact.

*   *

"Finished my shift! Can I get paid now?"

"Yes, yes. Here's your minced meat, bread, and corn. I made sure to give you the fatty bits of meat. Oh, and I put your take-home portion in a bag, so it'll be easier for you to carry."

"Whoa, now that's what I call service! All right, I'll be back tomorrow to work hard some more!"

The crow began to eat with glee. Many of its comrades were already eating nearby, and take-home bags were lined up next to them.

If I take this home, my wife and child won't have anything to complain about. What a great job... or, rather, a great feeding place... I found.

The crow hoped this gig would go on for some time, but didn't expect whoever lived in that house to be able to hold out much longer. Besides, there would be more tasks to do, starting tomorrow.

I'll have to work more from tomorrow, but it sounds like fun. The food is supposedly going to get better, so I say bring it on!

Then came the pack of dogs, led by three dogs at the front.

"Good work today! Go ahead and eat your fill. I'll see you again tomorrow!"

The three dogs at the head of the pack ignored the food and walked up next to the girl.

The rest of the dogs bowed their heads, then began eating. Unlike the ones stuffing their faces without a care in the world, the three dogs next to the girl had rather intense expressions on their faces. Indeed, it was as if they stood before a big bear in order to protect their master from harm.

I had hired the three house dogs, the freely roaming dogs that lived in the area, and other stray dogs, by offering them food. Some of them agreed on the condition that I relay a message they really wanted to tell their owners, or in exchange for me curing an injury or illness. And so, they were all more than happy to work for me. A doctor who could speak to animals...

Yes, I was a regular Doctor Dolittle.

Some time ago, that name was abridged to "Doctor Doritoru" because they figured the original would be too hard to pronounce for Japanese children, but it's actually "Do-little." Though, the Japanese spelling wasn't always consistent. Then, I realized something.

Speaking of "Doolittle," I needed to have some bombers. I couldn't just load a bunch of military bombers onto an aircraft carrier, but I needed something... And that's when I scouted the crows.

They wouldn't run away even if you got close enough to talk to them, and they were great at intimidation, with all that creepiness and intensity. Plus, they ate just about anything, so providing incentives would be a piece of cake. They were perfect!

Animals that only ate bugs or living creatures, or were hard to find, or didn't let you get close enough to talk to them, could be a real pain to work with. Although, it would have been cooler if I could have gotten birds of prey like eagles, hawks, or falcons. But this time, I was going for the intimidation factor rather than coolness, so it was fine.

I'd have the crows work on dropping poop bombs all over the place. They'd been level bombing up till now, but starting tomorrow, I asked them to add dive-bombing into the mix. In exchange, I was giving them fruits, walnuts, and acorns as an additional reward.

*   *

"Ah! Damn it, get away!"

Anyone who visited that house fell victim to the dive-bombing crows. Not only did they get hit by their poop bombs, but their belongings were stolen, and their hands were scratched whenever they tried to block the pesky birds.

With such ongoing incidents, it became widely known that anyone who visited that house was a target, prompting a sense of anxiety and distrust among those visitors. A murder of crows would consider you their enemy... And, although they didn't directly harm visitors, numerous dogs sat and stared at anyone who got close. If they attacked like the crows were doing, it would be serious trouble for the visitors.

With these thoughts in mind, visiting merchants and delivery workers refused to enter the house, and their superiors didn't reprimand them for their refusal. Getting involved with that house meant trouble. That was the consensus among the local business owners.

Of course, the crow attacks weren't limited to visitors, but also the residents living in the house in question.

"Damn it, what the hell is going on?! What's with the dogs and crows...?"

Upon further investigation, it seemed that no one had been scattering food around the premises, after all.

Thinking that the smell might be the issue, Aragorn hired workers to clean at night while the dogs and crows were gone, and even placed herbs that had a scent that dogs hated, but it had absolutely no effect. Then, the crows that had just surrounded the house before became more aggressive with their harassment, and there was no telling when the dogs would join in.

"There's no way anyone could control dogs and crows. Besides, if such a power did exist, they could use it to become filthy rich. They could use the animals for shows, or make them work in the military... What would be the point of harassing me with it?! I never even did anything to deserve such treatment! This has to be supernatural in nature, but it's not like it's some sort of divine punishment..."

Aragorn flinched. Divine punishment... Had he done anything to deserve such a thing? He thought about it.

Would murdering his brother and his brother's wife and son for the family estate, then tricking the surviving niece into marrying him, be worthy of punishment in the eyes of the Goddess...? The Goddess was a woman, so perhaps she would have little mercy for those with malicious intent towards little girls.

Well, he may have already harbored guilt for killing his brother's family... But Celestine had no interest in crimes committed by humans, and she would never get involved in such a thing. That is, unless it led to mass murder on a grand scale, or some other catastrophe. Or, if someone was using her name to commit evil or did something to otherwise tarnish her name, that is. But no one besides Kaoru knew that.

The general populace understood from experience that the Goddess Celestine was quite careless, and didn't mind if bystanders were hurt in the process of dishing out divine punishment. But due to her appearance and gentle way of speech, they presumed that she was generally a benevolent goddess who struck down evil and upheld justice, but also happened to be bad at controlling her powers.

…Despite the fact that she had never done such a thing before.

"W-Wait a minute… It can't be… But if it is divine punishment, she'd just drop a lightning bolt on me, instead of doing it in such a roundabout way. So the Goddess has nothing to do with this! There must be another reason…"

Indeed, punishment delivered by Celestine would be swift and deadly. She wouldn't waste her time with harassment like this. In that sense, Aragorn's conjecture was correct. Although, really, that would do nothing to help him resolve his current predicament.

* *

"Count Maslias should be hearing the rumors any time now…"

"Yes, his subordinates and retainers may hesitate to report such rumors to him directly, but now that they're so widespread, the count himself or someone close to him should hear of them, and will likely give an order to look into the details," Emile responded as such to Kaoru's comment.

Count Maslias's house was the parent house of House Raphael. As a weaker noble house that wasn't particularly wealthy, House Raphael was part of a faction, in which Count Maslias was an influential figure. The house of Count Maslias was in a neighboring territory, so it had acted as House Raphael's protector for generations. Of course, they received tribute in return, and House Raphael was expected to side with Count Maslias if they were ever at odds over national policies with other factions.

In other words, House Raphael could not oppose House Maslias. The current Count Maslias was a man of character, who took care of the lower nobles of his retainer houses and treated them with kindness. He even loved the children of Viscount Raphael, Mariel and her older brother, as if they were his own.

Kaoru had heard this from Mariel herself, when she had asked the young girl if there was anyone other than the king who could step in and punish criminals, and might also be on her side.

"Hmhmhm, soon…"

An evil grin spread across Kaoru's face.

"What's 'soon'?"

"Eep!"

Francette's voice spoke up from behind, and Kaoru let out a yelp in surprise.

"Oh, um, n-nothing! I was saying, dinner will probably be ready soon…"

That was bad. Clearly a bad attempt at an excuse.

"…I see. I thought you were just preparing to dice up some meat scraps to feed the crows again."

Kaoru and Emile froze.

"Did you think I wouldn't notice? Haah… I would stop you if you were putting yourself in danger, but otherwise, I won't try to stop you or get in the way. In fact, if you are working as a goddess, it would be my duty to aid you. I wish you would trust… or, rather, put… your servants to use more…"

With that, Francette shot Emile a glare.

It seemed that she didn't like the fact that she had been kept out of the loop while Emile was part of the plan. After all, Francette had met Kaoru first, and she would likely be unhappy with the fact that she, a knight who had sworn loyalty to Kaoru, was considered to be below a novice like Emile. Her swordsmanship being judged was one thing, but to think her loyalty was seen as less than Emile's…

"Oh, Roland..." Kaoru began.

"Sir Roland is royalty. He cannot be involved in matters regarding nobles of other countries," Francette replied, cutting her off.

Kaoru was thinking:

Francette is a noble too, so wouldn't it be problematic for her to get involved with matters regarding nobles of other countries too?

Besides, regardless of whether you're royalty, a noble, or a commoner, wouldn't sticking your neck in such business be an issue anyway...?

*　　　*

"Is this true?!"

Count Maslias, the current head of the parent house of House Raphael, shouted to his subordinate. He couldn't believe the report he had just heard.

"Yes, my lord. I heard the servants speaking of such rumors, and when I investigated the residence of Aragorn von Raphael, it was just as they said... When I approached the gate with a small bag in hand, the, ah... crow, defecated directly on me, and my bag was knocked out of my hand. As the bag landed on the ground, it was torn to shreds by a pack of dogs. It was clearly a coordinated and deliberate act, and one that doesn't seem possible for a human to orchestrate..."

"So that's why there are rumors of him committing a heinous act that brought divine punishment upon him. The only atrocity related to Viscount Raphael that occurred as of late would be..."

The answer was obvious.

"I cannot have Mariel marry patriarch-murdering scum! And, of course, such a man is not fit to be the head of House Raphael.

Even if His Majesty and the Goddess allow it, I… Well, I suppose the Goddess doesn't allow it, which is why this is happening. Seeing as she has yet to strike him down with lightning, this must be her way of saying he must be judged by the hands of men. And if we were to ignore her wishes…"

The stories of past incidents regarding the Goddess Celestine's wrath crossed the minds of Count Maslias and his men. The incidents that ended up involving countless innocents in the vicinity…

"We must head to House Raphael tomorrow morning! Send a messenger right away. Send a messenger to Aragorn as well, ordering him to go to House Raphael!"

"Yes, my lord!"

They would be going to Raphael Manor rather than Aragorn's house because Aragorn had no title or servants, and his home was no place to host a meeting. Even if that weren't the case, no one wished to go to an unclean house that had been stricken by the wrath of the Goddess.

*   *

"Count Maslias will be visiting tomorrow morning."

"I see. That was quicker than I thought."

It was late at night, and Kaoru was sipping tea at Raphael Manor and having a meeting with Mariel. Everyone in House Raphael already knew Kaoru was no ordinary human, and treated her with the respect due someone far above their own station.

"Tomorrow morning, so the second morning bell…" Kaoru muttered to herself.

In this region, saying "tomorrow morning" or "first thing tomorrow" in regards to work or meetings meant "at the second morning bell," which was 9 a.m. in Earth time. This was unusually early for a noble's house visit.

"He must have just heard the news today. I assume he is quite flustered…"

Mariel was probably right.

Around here, or rather, in most countries in this world, even though the people had great faith in and appreciation for the Goddess Celestine, they also contemplated her punishments with an incredible amount of fear and dread. This wasn't a fear of being punished due to one's own crimes. Rather…

This was a fear of "the Goddess Celestine being so careless that countless innocent citizens are inadvertently struck down by a stray bolt of her divine punishment, resulting in destruction on a national scale."

And so, despicable acts that could incur such a punishment were deserving of capital punishment, and no connections, bribes, status, or power could absolve those who committed them. This was just common sense. No one would possibly accept a paltry bribe in exchange for the destruction of the nation, along with their entire clan.

"So, this will all be settled tomorrow morning…"

With that, Kaoru smiled a smile that could make children cry. Behind her were Emile, Belle, and Francette. Layette was sleeping in Kaoru's lap.

Afterward, Emile and Belle disappeared into the night, and the others returned to their home base at the convenience store. They would sleep and rest well in preparation for the morning.

*   *

"Wh-Why are there so many people...?"

The following morning, Count Maslias of the parent house of House Raphael, along with his attendants, arrived at the Raphael residence to find a large crowd gathered there.

However, the crowd wasn't being rowdy or blocking the count's path, nor were they arguing with those who were standing by the public road. Count Maslias found it odd, but nevertheless stepped onto the premises of Raphael Manor. His attendant sounded the door knocker, at which point a butler promptly arrived to guide them in.

"Are you in good health, Mariel?"

The count had been very supportive of Mariel immediately after the incident, but some distance had grown between them after it had settled. However, no one could really blame him for it. He had been spending so much time trying to help Mariel that he had neglected his own territory, and was reproached by his retainers as a result. Since then, he had been focusing on catching up on all the work that had piled up.

In Count Maslias's eyes, Mariel was indeed like his own daughter.

"Yes, I am doing fine. And there is something I must do, so there is no time for me to waste."

With that, her gaze turned toward Aragorn.

There were currently eight people in the room. On House Raphael's side were three people: Mariel, the butler, and the under-butler. However, the under-butler's clothes clearly didn't fit properly, and he seemed too physically developed to be a high-ranking servant. He lacked an air of intellect and dignity. It was quite plain to see that he was a guard in disguise. This was likely in the event that Aragorn decided to resort to brute force, in which case Mariel would be too weak to stop him, and the old butler might not be too reliable in a fight.

As for Aragorn, he was by himself. He wouldn't need a guard simply to visit the house of his head family, or to visit Count Maslias of his parent house, and a poor, unmarried noble with no title like him didn't have any servants in the first place. If he went out of his way to hire guards just for this visit, it would be seen as an offense directed at the count and the current head of House Raphael, and it would bring the gravity of the situation into question. To Aragorn, this wasn't a viable option.

Count Maslias had come with two guards. Guards usually remained on standby in another room, but this time they were on watch in here with them. This could be perceived as discourtesy, but he did hold the highest position here. Moreover, this was a welcome move in Mariel's perspective, as it put her more at ease. Aragorn had assumed that the count had come to bless his union with Mariel, or to discuss the ongoing relationship between House Raphael and House Maslias, so he thought nothing of it.

That made seven people. The final one was...

"A pleasure to make your acquaintance. I am Nagase... a detective."

"A detective?!"

Not wanting them to know her first name, Kaoru opted to refer to herself as "Nagase." She disliked lying needlessly, and wanted to avoid a situation where she raised suspicion by going by a completely different name and then failing to react to it in a timely manner.

And rather than her name, Aragorn and the count reacted to the unfamiliar word, "detective," by cocking their heads in confusion. Of course, she didn't use the actual Japanese word for "detective," but a new word she had coined based on a similar nuance in this nation's language.

"Indeed. One who investigates and detects the truth. A 'detective.'"

Count Maslias and Aragorn wondered why this person was there at all, but considering Mariel had gone out of her way to bring her, and from that introduction, the count surmised the purpose of Kaoru's attendance. As for Aragorn, he assumed this stranger was some sort of shrine maiden, there to perform the marriage ceremony between Mariel and himself.

"Now, let's get right to it."

Count Maslias took a seat and began the discussion, after only giving Mariel a brief greeting and without so much as a word to Aragorn. Mariel was the current head of House Raphael and the hostess of this meeting, while Aragorn was a member of a branch family and had no title, so this wasn't particularly discourteous, but Aragorn had a displeased look on his face, despite being in front of Count Maslias, as he already considered himself the head of House Raphael.

The count had taken notice, but completely ignored him. That was insignificant when considering what was about to happen.

"Aragorn, I hear you have been receiving the Goddess's divine punishment. The Goddess Celestine does not normally intervene in matters regarding individual humans. Just what sort of grave sin have you committed to deserve her judgment?! If you've incurred her wrath, you may have doomed this entire nation—no, the continent— along with yourself! Speak! What have you done?!"

"Wha..."

This was supposed to be the discussion to finalize the achievement of his ambitions, but instead, he had been unexpectedly denounced by the head of his parent house. Aragorn was stunned.

"I-It's nothing but a baseless rumor…"

"A rumor? But is your house not currently surrounded by crows and dogs, and do they not assault anyone who steps within the premises?"

"Th-That's because someone fed the animals, as a prank…"

Aragorn desperately tried to find an excuse, but Count Maslias was unrelenting.

"The crows and dogs acted with coordination, accurately picking out their targets. Are you claiming a human could possibly pull off such a feat? Aragorn, do you truly believe the things you're saying right now?"

"…"

Aragorn grew quiet, unable to muster a retort. Even he knew that this couldn't have possibly been the work of a human being. However, even though he had been worried at first, he didn't believe that this was really divine punishment.

"B-But the Goddess Celestine has never punished men in such a roundabout way! In the past, she has always destroyed entire towns and nations with powerful lightning strikes, whirling infernos, tidal waves, fissures, or other cataclysms. And the last time she did so was several hundred years ago. Again, no matter what sort of crime has been committed, the Goddess has never judged an individual's deeds or meddled with human affairs! She's not concerned with the laws humans make for themselves, and the only time she's really angered is when someone tarnishes the Goddess's name, or uses it for their own selfish gain, or wreaks havoc on nature on a large scale…"

"What...?"

Count Maslias gave him a dubious look at first, which then turned to one of exasperation.

"You claim the last divine punishment was several hundred years ago... This has never been officially announced, but you do realize that there have been rumors spreading not just among nobles, but to the common people, through the priests and the merchants?"

"Huh? What are you talking about?"

Aragorn was perplexed by the count's response. Then, the count replied with a grave tone.

"The last time the Goddess brought divine punishment down upon the land was a little over four years ago. I'm sure you, too, have heard of these events: The defeat of the Aligot Empire's invading army and the destruction of the Holy Land of Rueda..."

"Wha..."

Aragorn was lost for words for just a moment, then fiercely argued back.

"The ones responsible for defeating the Aligot Empire's forces were the guardian of the Kingdom of Balmore, 'Fearsome Fran,' and her subordinates, the 'Grim Reapers'! Then the Goddess descended upon the peace conference to convince the others to end the conflict..."

Count Maslias shook his head.

"That's inaccurate information spread by the commoners. According to the report directly from the delegation attending the peace conference,

"'The empire's forces invading from the western region were repelled by Fearsome Fran's party, and the Goddess sent her Angel to face the forces invading from the north. As a result, the Kingdom of Balmore sustained very few casualties and successfully captured all enemy soldiers.'

"Also, 'The Goddess descended upon the peace conference to state that the Holy Land of Rueda would be annihilated. But thanks to the Angel's pleading to spare the populace, the Goddess contained herself to the destruction of the rotten priests.'

"In other words, it has only been slightly more than four years since the last time the Goddess expressed her wrath, and it is likely that she has changed her method from direct punishments to indirect punishments, such as through another medium entirely. Perhaps she does it to bully— No, no, entertain— I mean, due to some change in her state of mind…"

Aragorn stood frozen, but he soon recovered and began defending himself again.

"I-I've done nothing to deserve this! And I haven't been accused of a crime!"

Aragorn had hired "Black Ops" for the hit. Government intelligence organizations often had their own secret units to handle illicit or immoral operations, such as murder and kidnapping, but this was an illegal and private organization unrelated to the government groups. It consisted of former high-ranking hunters, those who had been banished, those who had been fired by their nation's intelligence organization due to a highly problematic personality, and those who had fled from the intelligence organizations of other nations.

These individuals were highly skilled and fiercely loyal to their criminal organization, largely out of necessity, so they were "reliable criminals" who kept secrets and contracts at all costs. This was the private crime organization known as Black Ops.

He had little concern that the secret had been leaked, considering they were the ones who handled the entire job. It was nothing like hiring any random group of thugs or outlaw hunters. Aragorn knew he was under suspicion for "the incident," but with no accusers and no proof to be had, he was confident that even the parent house couldn't make a move against him, given that he was the heir to a noble house.

However...

"Someone has already stepped forward with an accusation."

"Wha..."

Mariel, who had been quiet until now, suddenly dropped that bomb of a comment.

"Uncle... No, Aragorn, the monster who plotted to take over my house by murdering the head of House Raphael and his entire family! I said someone has cast a formal suit against you!"

Mariel's smiling face had transformed into an expression of pure anger, and even Count Maslias, along with Aragorn, couldn't hide his expression of shock. The only ones who were unaffected by the sudden change were the members of Viscount Raphael's household and the mysterious girl.

"I-Impossible! Who, what proof..."

"Proof? No such thing is needed. After all, they directly witnessed the incident with their own eyes. They saw you happily chatting with the individuals you hired to murder my father, mother, and brother!!!"

Aragorn was completely motionless, and Count Maslias was stunned. The count had come prepared to denounce Aragorn, but he hadn't expected Mariel, who had already agreed to marry her uncle, to denounce him herself with such intensity. In fact, he didn't think she had prepared at all for this moment, much less gone as far as to find witnesses.

"Then I'd like to see them! You'd better be prepared for the consequences if this is some sort of lie!" Aragorn roared back, and Mariel shot him down with an icy cold tone.

"Of course. And Aragorn! You dare speak so to the mistress of your head family, yourself a mere untitled man of a branch house, and in the presence of Count Maslias of your parent house? Have you no shame?!"

"Urgh…" Aragorn turned red with humiliation, but he couldn't act out further in front of Count Maslias.

Considering how events had transpired, it was unlikely that Mariel would willingly marry him now, even if he somehow managed to talk his way out of this situation. However, if Aragorn claimed that Mariel had gone insane with grief after losing her family, he could potentially force her to give up her inheritance, leaving him as the new head of the house.

Aragorn quickly collected himself after coming to this conclusion. There was no way anyone could have witnessed the event, after all. It had happened on a public street corner, and his men were standing watch to make sure that no witnesses had been around to see anything. And judging by how she phrased it, as someone having "witnessed the incident," it would be safe to assume it wasn't someone from the Black Ops organization. This meant she had hired someone to provide false testimony. He could still get through this.

It was only natural for Aragorn to think this way.

"Well then, please follow me, everyone."

"Huh?"

Aragorn and Count Maslias looked rather perplexed as Mariel stood up.

"You wish to see the witness, correct? Please, this way." All they could do was follow.

They all stood and the seven of them followed Mariel out of the room, at which point the guards posted in the room next door followed after them. Francette was among them, of course. There was no way she would let Kaoru enter enemy territory alone. She had been listening in along with the House Raphael and House Maslias guards, ready to burst through the door as soon as something went wrong.

*   *

Emile and Belle went into the city after they had parted with Kaoru and the others the previous evening. Not to enjoy the nightlife, of course, but to provide publicity.

They went around the Hunter's Guild headquarters, the taverns, and other areas, spreading the following rumor, "Tomorrow, at the second morning bell, witness a miracle before the house of Viscount Raphael."

And this morning, they woke up at the first morning bell (around six in the morning) to go around the common wells and morning markets to spread the same message.

Nobody stopped to question it, what with the rumors of House Raphael's branch family's "divine punishment" being so widespread. In this world, no one was foolish enough to doubt the existence of the Goddess or her judgment.

Afterward, Emile and Belle went to the stables where Ed and the other horses were being kept, then brought them out, claiming that they were needed for work. Of course, this included the newest of Kaoru's horses, Carlos.

The horses would do as ordered, even without Emile and Belle escorting them, but if horses were seen roaming about without humans around, they would be at risk of being stolen by scoundrels or turned over to a guard post or guild by some well-meaning person.

Emile and Belle were sent to escort the horses to avoid such a situation, but they simply walked alongside the horses, without riding them. This was a key point: the horses had to move of their own will, without humans riding them. They walked on for a short time after leaving the stable, then stopped. Then, Emile and Belle placed masks on the six horses. The six horses began walking again.

After some time, a group of dogs joined them from the left and right sides of the intersection. Several more joined at the next intersection. And more at the next. And more at the one after. The horses increased their pace to a fast walk. Emile, Belle, and the dogs increased their own pace to keep up.

From intersecting side streets... Back alleys... Eaves of residential houses...

Dogs, dogs, dogs, dogs...

Dogs came running. Dogs came to join them.

Then, when the second morning bell rang throughout the city...

Crows came flying in out of nowhere, as if they had been waiting for the signal.

Crows, crows, crows, crows...

And so, the tanks (dogs) advanced forward, leading the fighter-bombers (crows) flying overhead. Along with the six horses...

In search of their prey.

"Where in the world are we going...?" Aragorn was expecting this so-called witness to be in another room, but Mariel led them through the front door, out of the manor, and toward the front gates. Despite his complaints, he had no choice but to follow. Count Maslias and the guards from both houses continued following, as well.

Behind them was a line of House Raphael's servants. Butlers, cooks, maids, coachmen, gardeners, footmen, porters... and all the rest of the servants were in tow, their expressions hard. They all wore the same stoic look on their faces, as if they were barely containing a whirlwind of emotions. Only their eyes betrayed an intense, eerie glow.

Mariel walked a few meters out from the gate, then stopped.

There, a large crowd, having gathered from all over town, stood waiting.

"..."

The members of House Raphael and the girl seemed unfazed by the crowd before them.

On the other hand, Aragorn, Count Maslias, and the count's guards looked rather tense. They had no idea why there was a crowd gathered there. What if they had some sort of grudge against House Raphael and suddenly turned violent? They had far too few guards to hold off an attack from a crowd of such a size. Cold sweat ran down their backs as the thought crossed their minds.

But even then, they didn't allow their nervousness to show on their faces. As nobles, they could never show panic or seem undignified in front of commoners, even if they *were* straining to keep up a front.

"H-Hmph, are you saying your witness is someone in this crowd? Don't tell me you're going to claim that they're all going to testify. This is a mere intimidation tactic, and seeing as you have to resort to this, you clearly have no proof, and..."

"Witnesses, please step forward," Mariel raised her voice, speaking over the flustered Aragorn, and the crowd parted to let six horses through.

However, these six weren't Ed and his crew, but the two riding horses and four carriage horses owned by House Raphael. Of course, these horses wore no masks. The six horses wore no saddle and were pulling no carriage, and were led by a coachman and horsekeeper, who were also on foot, stopping just in front of Mariel. Aragorn looked around in search of a rider who had dismounted from the horses, but there weren't any people there besides the men leading the horses and the crowd around them.

"What witness…"

Mariel cut him off and shouted, "Who is the one who hired the killers to murder my parents and brother?"

Then, each of the horses raised their front right leg and pointed… directly at Aragorn.

"The horses are the witnesses?!" Aragorn and Count Maslias shouted in unison.

Then, Count Maslias continued, "You were talking about horses this entire time…?"

But everyone ignored the question.

Why had the horses pointed at Aragorn in response to Mariel's words? The reason was simple: Kaoru had taught them several patterns to perform in response to Kaoru's signals. The horses had simply reacted to Kaoru's gesture of pointing at Aragorn while bending her hand at the wrist in front of her stomach.

This had all been explained prior to this meeting, so they all understood what this event was for. The signals were simply for supporting Mariel as she made her case.

Upon seeing this, the crowd reacted.

"Ooooooohhh!"

"The horses are denouncing their master's killer!"

"An ordinary horse couldn't do this! This is the work of the Goddess! The Goddess Celestine was moved by the girl's will to seek vengeance and the loyalty of the horses, and decided to lend them her strength!"

Aragorn turned pale as the crowd continued to shout.

"…Well? What do you have to say?"

Count Maslias expected Aragorn to back down then and there. Now that the Goddess Celestine was said to be involved, there was no way for him to escape punishment for his crimes, after all.

"Whatever do you mean? An impertinent child taught her pet horses a little trick. That's all there is to it. What's more, she's a vile little fiend who seeks to frame her noble uncle with underhanded tactics! She is a disgrace to the nobility, and should be stripped of her title and exec—"

Plop!

"…Huh?"

Aragorn felt as if something had fallen on his head and put a hand there to check.

"Bird… droppings?"

Plop! Plop! Plop plop plop…

"Whoa, whoa, whoa!"

Confused, Aragorn looked up to find a sight that was all too familiar at his residence as of late…

The sight of fighter-bombers (crows), flying in units.

"Look, the Goddess's familiars…"

"Give it up already, or the Goddess will strike you down!"

"I hear the Goddess Celestine isn't the best at aiming, so we— No, the entire nation could end up going down with you! Confess already!!!"

The crowd grew louder, but if he confessed now, he would certainly be beheaded. After all, he would be admitting to murdering the head of a noble house, along with that head's wife and heir, all so he could take over. The crime was even more grave than being an arsonist or a thief.

"N-No! So what if a few crows came here looking for food?! The Goddess has no interest in human affairs... I-I mean, she must have sent them to denounce that girl's evil deeds! The crows are really after House Raphael, and she's the current head of House Raphael. I just happened to be here today, and..."

But Aragorn's desperate excuses didn't convince anyone, seeing as the only one being targeted by crows and being pelted with dung was Aragorn himself.

Just then, one end of the rowdy crowd suddenly fell silent. Then the silence spread through the rest of the crowd. The crowd parted from the back, the dividing line extending all the way to the front and toward House Raphael's gates.

Through that new path walked six masked horses, followed by tens of dogs, dogs, dogs...

Clop, clop, clop.

Clop, clop, clop, clop, clop...

One in the front. One each on either side behind it. And three behind them in the third row. The six horses walked along in an arrowhead formation. At the front was, of course...

"Carlos!!!"

There was no way Mariel wouldn't recognize him, even with the mask on. It was Carlos, Mariel's personal riding horse that she had known for so long. Her beloved horse that she had heard was dead at one point, until the mysterious girl had informed her of his survival. But this was no time to be celebrating their reunion. The horse had to fulfill his role, as he had been instructed.

"The chief riding horse of House Raphael, Carlos! I commend you for seeking and finding the Goddess to send her my wishes! Now, along with the holy horses who have brought you here and the Goddess's familiars, the crows and dogs, please witness the conclusion to this ordeal!"

The horses neighed enthusiastically in response.

"Oooooohhh!"

It's over, Aragorn... Count Maslias thought to himself.

The horses, dogs, and crows haven't said a word. And no one really knows the truth of what happened. But with her own words, Mariel just "created" the truth. No one will question Mariel's words now, and no one will lend an ear to what Aragorn has to say...

Count Maslias was impressed by Mariel's execution.

She had always been a bright girl, but that was just compared to an average noble girl. He never expected her to connect the Goddess to a riding horse... And not to a soldier riding a horse, but the horse itself. In fact, one normally wouldn't think of such a thing, nor would they think it possible to pull off. If someone could have foreseen this result, they would be far from normal. Even if they ended up being right.

Perhaps I greatly underestimated Mariel... No, no, no!

Count Maslias quickly shook his head. No matter how clever she was, no human could have such a connection with the Goddess. Had she really ordered those horses to...?

No, I must use my common sense!

The count looked at the horses, dogs, and crows overhead, then hung his head...

Count Maslias actually didn't fully believe in Mariel's words himself. But there was no mistaking that there was something supernatural about these events. And whoever was responsible for these supernatural events was clearly on Mariel's side, and there wasn't anyone he could think of that would fit such a profile, besides the Goddess Celestine herself. This went not just for the count, but everyone gathered there...

Having witnessed the once-in-a-lifetime event of an actual miracle, and the moment a beautiful noble girl avenged her family, the crowd was all worked up, undulating like a massive wave.

Seeing this, the count thought to himself: *I must ride this big wave!*

"Aragorn, just accept it."

But Aragorn wouldn't give up. If he confessed to his crimes now, he would lose far more than his reputation. Not only would he lose his status as a noble, he would be executed, so he was obviously going to struggle until the very end.

"A-Accept what? That girl has joined forces with the devil and murdered her own parents, then used her demonic connections to frame me for her own sins! She's the one we should be punishing, as the enemy of the Goddess..."

The count cringed visibly.

"It seems you misunderstand something."

"Huh?"

Aragorn paused after being cut off, and Count Maslias continued.

"I may be the count of your parent house, but I cannot simply do as I wish to a noble of another house. Unless they try to harm me directly, that is. So, there's no point in you trying to make excuses to me, or trying to convince me of your innocence. Even His Majesty the King couldn't freely punish nobles without evidence. If he did, the nobles would revolt!"

"Ah, then...!"

Aragorn looked elated upon realizing Count Maslias didn't intend to convict him. But the count wasn't done talking.

"Whether there's evidence or not, the only one who can freely punish a noble is that noble's head of house."

"...What?"

Aragorn's neck turned slowly, laboriously, until it faced toward Mariel. There, he saw Mariel's face, smiling right at him.

At first, Mariel thought no one would ever listen to a child like her, even if she did speak up. Her brother was to be the heir, so Mariel hadn't received any education about being the head of house, and though she had been instructed on how to be a lady, those lessons had not included details on the dark side of managing a house, such as the head of house's right to freely deal with a family member as they wished.

But now, ever since she had resolved to get revenge, she had researched and studied everything she could possibly do.

"Mariel doesn't need evidence or witnesses to sentence you. She can simply say you disobeyed the head of the house or brought shame upon the house in order to strip you of your nobility, lock you in a dungeon for life, or even behead you. The reason she has gone through this entire procedure is to prove that it wasn't some ordinary bandits who got the best of her parents, and to show the public that she had finally avenged her family's killer. With the lone heiress getting revenge for her family, and with the full support of her house, she not only avoids losing face or her title, but she has all but ensured her stability as the head of the noble family that is watched over by the Goddess Celestine. Who would dare make a move on the noble family that has the favor of the Goddess herself? If such a fool exists, I'd like to meet them."

Count Maslias then turned to Mariel, ignoring Aragorn completely as he collapsed to the ground.

"What will you do with him? I presume it would be difficult to see his face if he was kept alive. Someone could plot to use him somehow, as well. Shall I take care of him?"

Mariel shook her head.

"Thank you for your consideration. But as the head of my house, I must be the one to get rid of my family's shame. I only need the Goddess's helping hand to guide me."

"I see… Yes, of course…"

That would be more effective for when the rumors spread among the nobles and in the royal palace. This way, she would be known as the fierce and dignified viscountess, favored by the Goddess, who avenged her parents and brother by her own hands.

The count couldn't help but nod repeatedly in understanding.

*   *

"…Well then, allow me to go over the final confirmation of the contract's details."

The event ended without us having to step in. Afterward, Mariel's servants tied up her uncle, Aragorn, and dragged him off to the dungeons… So, they really did have dungeons…

The count left after talking for some time, and we had just gone over the confirmation of the completed job.

Oh, Emile and Belle had taken Ed and the others back already, and the crows and dogs had dispersed, for now. They were all pretty disappointed, since they had had a pretty good gig going. They wanted me to contact them again next time, but I really doubted there would be all that many job opportunities for seeking revenge like this. Well, I did give it some thought, at least, for their sakes.

As for Carlos, he went straight to the stables here, got his mask off, and he'd been there ever since. Mariel already paid me the amount I bought him for.

…I wasn't running a charity, after all. I would be collecting expenses, separate from my retainer.

"I've received the retainer and expenses, so I'd like to discuss the bonus reward… As we discussed previously, I've permitted the crows and dogs one visit each to come to this house if they ever get injured, sick, or otherwise need help. If a dog or crow enters your premises looking weak, please protect them and provide care and food. Then, I ask that you keep records of their visit and turn them away if they return a second time. Likewise, if they come simply to beg for food."

"…"

Mariel and the butler had rather awkward looks on their faces.

Well, if they wanted to provide service for the second visits and so on, that was up to them. I was just pointing out that their responsibility, as stated by the contract, was to treat them just the once.

"Dogs are one thing, but we wouldn't really be able to tell the crows apart. Even if we had portraits of each one…"

Oh.

The butler nodded in agreement at Mariel's rather astute point.

Urrrgh…

"I-I'll leave that up to you…"

If a crow ever got injured, they would most likely die then and there. I didn't expect a lot of them to be able to make it to the mansion. Yes, I'll leave it all up to them! It's their problem now!

And so, everything had been fully resolved. The initial job as the "animal doctor," the additional horse translations, and the final assistance with her revenge...

The revenge case was technically a request from Carlos, but with all the extra requests that came afterward, I had signed a new contract with Mariel to consolidate the additional issues. Otherwise, all that crow and dog food would have put me wholly in the red. It wasn't like Carlos was going to pay me, after all.

"Well then, I'll be going now..."

"Please wait!"

Just as I tried to leave along with Francette, who was waiting in the back, Mariel called out to me.

"...Yes?" I stopped walking and asked, then Mariel and the butler rose from their seats, and they, along with the servants who had been waiting behind them, got on their hands and knees and bowed their heads toward me.

"We sincerely thank you for your help, from the bottom of our hearts. If possible, please, we ask that you give us an opportunity to repay you..."

Ahh... I didn't really want to deal with that kind of thing... But it would've been rude of me to tell Mariel that, I guess...

"Yes, if such an opportunity ever arises..." I said, mostly to be polite, as I prepared to leave for real this time... But wait, why did that servant girl look so worried?

"What is it?"

"Ah! N-No, it's nothing!"

Yeah, that was the expected response.

"Tell me!"

"Eeeeeek!!!"

Wow, she didn't have to get that scared... Wait, is it the eyes?! Are my eyes that scary?!

No, no, I had used adhesive to force my eyes to look droopier and used makeup to cover it up.

...So what's the deal?!

"Speak!"

"Y-Y-Yes! U-Um, is it okay to say the crows and dogs that helped us are servants of the Goddess...? We won't really incur the wrath of the Goddess this time, will we...?"

Oh, that. She thought I was just some girl who could speak to animals, so she was afraid I was using the Goddess's name for my own gain. Her concerns were completely understandable, considering that this was Celes we were dealing with.

"Don't worry. Celes wouldn't get angry over such a minor thing, and she wouldn't complain about something I decided to do. Because..."

"Because?"

"Celes and I are friends!"

Some of the other servants looked anxious too, so I figured it'd be fine to tell them, just to put their minds at ease. I'd already stressed to Mariel and all the serving staff that they were to speak of me to absolutely no one.

The servants were flabbergasted, though Mariel and the butler must have already suspected this, as they were rather unperturbed.

I left the house of Viscount Raphael behind with Francette, who seemed dissatisfied by the way I had been in the background during the earlier events, but she was full of smiles after seeing me being worshiped in the end.

*   *

"...So that's what happened."

After dinner, Francette gave the full account of what had happened up until now to Roland. He needed to have this information, just in case something related to this incident came up later on, making this a necessary process.

"Why was I left out of this?!"

...Even though we knew Roland would get upset.

"That is, of course, because we cannot have you, a member of the royal family, getting involved with issues concerning nobles of another nation. If you happened to let slip your own status, or the need for you to reveal your identity were to arise, it would have led to an international incident..."

"Then how about you, Francette? You're a noble of our own kingdom! That could have led to an international incident, too, could it not?!"

Yeah... I figured he'd say that... Honestly, I probably would have argued the same thing.

But Francette was unperturbed.

"In that case, I would simply have forfeited my title as viscountess and instead become a vagabond swordswoman in exile. I would have you return to the kingdom, and our engagement would be null and void..."

"Wha?! Fran, you would go that far...?"

She would have given up her nation, family, and engagement, becoming a wanderer without a home. But as Roland was greatly admiring her spirit...

"Then, as the guardian knight of the goddess, I would spend my days happily with the four of us: me, Lady Kaoru, Layette, and Belle... Hehe, hehehe..."

"What? That was your true intention?!"

"Where am I in your plan?!"

Roland yelled, and Emile raised his own objection, as Francette drooled with a slovenly smile, lost in her fantasies.

Yeah, I figured as much...

Besides, what nation would dare exile Fearsome Fran, the reborn knight, the great hero who had been granted the divine blade and received the blessing of the Goddess? They would rather risk a war than lose someone like her. In fact, they might even prioritize her over Roland. No, seriously...

* *

"An emissary from the royal palace has arrived."

"Let them through."

It was finally time.

An emissary from the royal palace...

"Not to worry, I've already sent a letter to His Majesty. This is likely just for confirmation."

With that, Count Maslias gave me a reassuring look. He had taken good care of me and House Raphael since even before my family's passing, and I admired him greatly. He had come here hurriedly today purely out of concern for me, immediately upon hearing the news of the emissary's upcoming arrival. With my parents no longer here, he was like a father to me.

...An emissary from the royal palace.

Indeed, the visit was to confirm the truth about the death of my family, my uncle Aragorn's crimes, and how he had been dealt with, all of which I'd detailed in a letter to His Majesty the King.

Count Maslias informed me that he had also explained the circumstances in a letter, and as such he assured me that this was merely a formality to confirm the details...

I greeted the emissary in the reception room and began explaining the situation, though everything had already been outlined in the letter, so there wasn't much to add.

"So, what happened to the divine horses, crows, and dogs of the Goddess that this horse, Carlos, brought in?"

"Huh? I had them leave, of course."

The emissary, surprisingly, was a count. I had been expecting a common government official, or perhaps a third- or fourth-born noble of lower rank, one that was perhaps an untitled civil servant. And he did not question me about my uncle... no, Aragorn's... crimes, but focused on the details of the unnatural phenomena... or, rather, the Goddess's miracles. I took this to mean that they had no intention of meddling with the internal affairs of House Raphael, or how I had handled Aragorn's disposal. Although, really, it wasn't as if I had done anything worthy of reprimand in the first place.

If they had interfered with the legitimate head of a noble house punishing a villain within their own family, the other nobles would end up fearing that the same thing could happen to them and would likely stand together against the royal family. The current royal family had a relatively good relationship with the powerful noble houses, so it was unlikely that they would do something so foolish, especially when they would not benefit from going after a small viscountcy like mine.

Besides, the royal family should have been aware that Count Maslias wouldn't idly stand by and let such a thing happen. Which meant that House Raphael should be safe, but...

"...And did you happen to meet a young girl with scary eyes as of late?"

Huh?

What was this about? The one I met had kindly, downturned eyes. Though, there was an unnaturalness about her face, like it was being pulled taut.

"No, no one like that..."

"I-I see. Then what about, o-oh, I don't know, someone who could perform miracles from the Goddess...?"

"As I mentioned previously, the only mysterious events were the actions of the crows, dogs, and horses."

"I see... Then, would you mind letting me meet those horses?"

"Oh, um, sure, that's not a problem..."

When I brought him to the stables, Carlos and the other horses walked over right away. I'd always been close with the horses, but I'd been even closer with them since that day.

"Carlos. I've heard of your great deeds. His Majesty was quite impressed, as well!"

"Brr? Bff!"

Ah, Carlos is blowing air out of his nose in annoyance, probably because an unfamiliar human is talking to him so presumptuously.

"Whoa!"

Oh, Carlos got a bit of snot on him...

The emissary asked me a few more things afterward, but he never ended up faulting me or those of House Raphael for what had happened, and left these words by the king before leaving: "You've done well. Continue to protect your house, your territory, and your people, and faithfully serve your kingdom."

"You carried yourself well, Mariel! This means your actions have been fully, officially approved, and His Majesty has acknowledged you as the rightful heir of House Raphael. Though, I suppose that conclusion was never really in question. In any case, I'm glad things turned out smoothly. Now, you should thank your servants for their hard work, reward them with a half-day off and some extra spending money, and take some rest for yourself, as well. I'm sure you're exhausted from everything you've been through. Managing your health is part of your duty and job as the viscountess. Rest well."

He left soon after, perhaps because he thought I wouldn't be able to rest with him around.

*   *

After the count took his leave, I did as he recommended: distributed a small allowance and told the servants, except the guards, to take the rest of the day off and return before it was time to close the gates.

The cooks had been dismissed as well, so there wouldn't be anything for them to eat if they stayed. I told them as much, and they laughed awkwardly as they prepared to go out for the day. Of course, the funds I had given them were enough to have a fairly high-quality meal with plenty to spare. I called it a small amount, but it obviously wasn't mere pocket change. We might not be powerful, but we were a noble house, after all. A viscount's house at that, not just some baronial house! Now that I had some free time, I decided to go to the stables to pay Carlos a visit.

"Carlos! Thank you for everything. I couldn't have done it without you. If you hadn't gotten to know the divine horse and met Lady Celestine's goddess friend, I never would have been able to avenge my family and secure House Raphael's future. I can't thank you enough…"

"Brr, brrrr!"

"I'm sorry for turning down the Goddess's offer to give you the ability to speak to humans with her magical potion. I thought you wouldn't need it…"

"Breehehe, brrr."

"That's why…"

"Reehehe, brehehe!"

"Brethat's brehewhy, I brehehad herhehe brehegive mehehe thehe breheability to speheheak to brehanimals! It's far more convenient this way. Now, I can also talk to the other horses and dogs, as well as crows and stray… I mean, independent… dogs, and properly thank them for their help. It's perfect!"

"Brehehe, breeehehe!"

"Breeehe! Heheeebrehe, brrr!"

"Breehehehe!"

*   *

"…So, you're saying it was a normal horse that couldn't speak the human tongue. Did you think I would be satisfied with such a report?!"

"I'm sorry!"

This nation of Beliscas had a king and nobles, but it wasn't ruled by a single king, and national policy was made by a council of upper-class nobles. Moreover, merchants held much stronger sway here than in other kingdoms and empires. Of course, this did have its drawbacks, as well. Nobles, merchants, commoners, and of course, the royal family… they had all heard of the miracle that had occurred in a provincial seaside city.

It was a somewhat, no, an extremely dubious story, about a young girl of a small noble house being saved by the blessing of the Goddess, allowing her to avenge her family and protect her house. One would normally dismiss such a tale with a laugh, but the viscount's heir in question had sent a report outlining her full account of the event, which was then followed by a report... or, rather, a written submission of opinions... by the count of her parent house.

National policies couldn't be decided by the king alone, but he did have the authority to determine whether or not there was an issue with a legitimate heiress punishing a family member who had committed a crime. He was respecting the rights of a small noble house, so there was no way the other nobles would actually object.

...But this was no ordinary incident.

The Goddess's miracle! A beautiful, young, female head of a noble house who was blessed by the Goddess! And she was unmarried! The king couldn't give up such a juicy story to those grubby nobles. This was the perfect opportunity to take in the girl who had been blessed by the Goddess, in order to increase his royal power and authority.

At the same time, there was a very real risk of the nobles taking her as their own tool to further their own influence. Which is why the king immediately sent a count who supported the royal family to confirm the truth, but he had returned without any real results. It was only natural for him to be upset.

"I will need to make my next move... The nobles have surely heard the news by now. I must hurry..."

Chapter 34:
Hot Springs

"Let's go to the hot springs!"

"Yes!"

"Huh?"

"?"

Emile and Belle agreed to my suggestion without question or thought, pretty much by reflex alone. Roland and Francette responded inquisitively. As for Layette, it seemed she didn't even know what hot springs were.

"So, what's a 'hot spring'?"

You too, Emile and Belle?!

"Hot springs are where hot water flows out naturally, and it's good for health and beauty…"

"Let's go!"

I wasn't even done speaking, but Francette and Belle were fully on board.

So quick to respond…

And so, we decided to go on a hot springs trip.

…Roland's input? That was never even in consideration.

In any case, humans can't just be working all the time. We need to play every once in a while! And so, the staff of Convenience Store Belle, plus lodgers, were off on a company trip!

*   *

"So, this seems like the place…"

We looked up a place on the map, asked around at the Hunter's Guild and Commerce Guild, bought a drink to get some info from an old man who claimed to have traveled all over, and then finally arrived at our destination, Fire Dragon Mountain.

No, a dragon didn't actually live there. It was just called that due to the white smoke and heat billowing up locally, which meant it was highly likely to have some hot springs. Or maybe magma flowed here long ago, and that's where the "fire dragon" part of its name came from.

And so…

"Hot springs? Yeah, they're here."

Bingo.

I'd found it right away. That was anticlimactic…

"But I haven't heard from many people who've actually been there… It's pretty far."

I found this out when gathering information at a tavern… The first guy I spoke to explained that there were hot springs around, but they were also in a mountainous region far from town, and even if you went there to soak and relax your muscles, you'd be covered in sweat and sore all over from the walk back, so it was all rather pointless.

That made sense. But since we'd come this far, I couldn't just go home. And we weren't in a hurry, so we could just walk slowly and camp out on the way back. I always had my camping gear in my Item Box, anyway. Besides, maybe we would end up running into some other hot springs nearby.

Yeah, no problem!

And so, I bought some local food products as camouflage, stuffed them into a dummy bag, and off we went!

"Hmm, where is it…" I muttered to myself while wearing the sensor for detecting hot springs, the "Hot Springs Sensor."

The Hot Springs Sensor was actually the "Searcher," a glasses-shaped target-detecting device. I had just set the target to "hot springs" this time. A reusable, eco-friendly product.

But according to the Hot Springs Sensor, it seemed that there were no other hot springs around.

…So, we ended up going all the way to the hot springs that I had originally been told about. Though, really, I should have expected this. If there had been hot springs close by, the locals would have found them at some point in the last several hundred years. Since no one had found any, they obviously didn't exist…

We arrived there without getting lost, thanks to the Hot Springs Sensor, and set up the tents (that I'd produced from the Item Box, of course) next to the hot springs. One for the girls, one for the guys, a tent with just a roof for resting under, and a table set.

Setup was done by Francette, Emile, and Belle. Roland was useless… Though, honestly, that went for me too.

There were obviously no buildings around the hot springs, and so it was just a pool of hot water that was welling up from the ground. The hot water that overflowed cooled immediately, flowing down to the lower levels in a small stream. I didn't know if that led into some river or just got absorbed into the ground.

There was a man-made groove where water flowed down from the hot well, leading into a hollow in the stone. This was about four and a half mats in size, with water draining out of the other side and into a stream, and it was used as a tub.

In addition, normal mountain water, which seemed to be drawn from somewhere else, was flowing next to the tub, and the amount of water flowing into it could be adjusted by moving the partition board.

"Wow, this is really well made... Though, I guess this sort of ingenuity could be expected if it's been around for several hundred years... Okay, Roland and Emile, shoo for now."

"Yes, ma'am!"

"...All right."

Yeah, I didn't expect them to argue with that.

After they left, we all took off our clothes, and it was time for the hot springs!

"Hot, hot, hot, hot, hot!!!"

When I stuck my right foot into the tub, I leapt into the air from the sheer heat.

...It obviously wasn't going to be the right temperature, considering that no one had adjusted it beforehand. I might even have died if I'd jumped right in. It would have been pretty pathetic if my second life ended because I got boiled alive in a hot spring.

I closed the partition board on the hot water, then opened the side with the cold water, and waited. It seemed like it would take a while, but luckily, it wasn't too cold and there wasn't much wind, and with the heat coming from the water, it was manageable even while naked. We were planning on camping out for the day, anyhow, so there was no rush. It seemed like we could take our time, since Emile and Roland were probably off looking for animals or fruit to eat.

And so, the four of us were leisurely talking while naked, when...

Rustle... Three men suddenly appeared out of the bushes. Then they looked at us and froze.

"Kyaaaaaaaaa!!!"

Screams filled the air.

…From the men.

Francette and I have both lived for about thirty years. I may not have had a boyfriend for just as long, but I wasn't going to screech in panic from kids seeing me naked at *my* age.

Belle had grown up in a deserted house full of boys and girls, with just one room to provide any shelter from the weather. Layette still didn't understand any of that stuff.

In my eyes, I supposed these kids were "men," but by the standards of the people here, they were probably only about thirteen to fourteen years old. They just happened to have bigger bodies. Basically, they were just "boys."

And before the three of them stood Francette, brandishing the divine sword Exgram, which had been placed nearby, high above her head… naked.

In any case… "Kyaaa"?

They sounded pretty girly…

"What happened?!"

"Are you all right, Lady Kaoru?!"

Roland and Emile appeared.

I guess they would, huh…

"Gyaaaaaaaaaa!!!"

This time, it was Francette and me who screamed.

Yeah, even we couldn't keep our cool about Roland seeing us naked.

But even though Francette was screaming, she had to maintain her position to defend us, so she just stood there, trembling, face bright red.

…But our instinctive yell was "Gyaaa."

We were so not *girly…*

And didn't Roland and Emile appear a little *too* quickly? Where had they been this whole time?!

*   *

"…So, you're from a nearby village?"

"Y-Yeah, we live in the village over that way. We come here once in a while…"

It was a bit far from the town, but apparently, there was a village nearby. The boys explained that they were residents there.

Well, the village was on the opposite side from the town where we'd learned about the hot springs, so I guess there was no reason for the townsfolk to mention it. There were probably other towns on the village's side of the hot springs, so there probably weren't a lot of opportunities for them to interact.

…Oh, and I'd already gone back to the girls' tent to put on some clothes, of course. We would've been too flustered to have a conversation, otherwise.

"Well, now that you're here, why don't you go in after us? It's not like the hot springs belong to us. In fact, the people from your village are the ones who have been maintaining them, so *we're* probably the ones in *your* way… It's probably supposed to be a mixed bath, but that's a little… you know. So, I'm gonna have to ask you to wait."

The boys nodded. I felt bad about making them wait, but in this case, I'd say it was definitely first come, first served. I mean, we wanted to go in first. These boys could go in later, with Roland and Emile. That way, it wouldn't be like we forced them out.

…But the villagers probably used this place as a mixed bath, so I wondered why they had freaked out when they saw us naked.

177

Could it be that they were surprised by how flat I was…?

Hey, shut up!

Curious, I asked them about it, and they turned bright red. Ah, so young… I thought, then realized they were looking at Francette and Belle.

Is it my chest? My eyes? …Both? Damn it! Wait, why was one of the three boys looking at Layette?! Wh-Why you… Don't tell me…

Oh, she just reminded him of his younger sister, from when he used to take care of her? I-I see…

And so, I let Roland and Emile keep watch on the boys, while the rest of us enjoyed the hot springs.

Oh, I know!

A lion-head-shaped container with a little bit of potion inside. Hot water that runs through it will absorb some of its nutrients, providing beautifying, healing, and relaxing properties. Appears perfectly fitted where the hot water comes out!

I pictured the details in my mind perfectly, so it'd work.

And it appeared, just as I imagined. You know, that lion head thing that spouts hot water from its mouth. Like it's barfing… Wait, that's actually kinda gross! No, not like barf! Anyway, the lion head was stuck to the stone, and water being poured into the back of the head came out of its mouth. It was just an ornament… or so it seemed.

We'd traveled all the way out here, so I wanted to do something a little nice for the always hard-working Francette. Every once in a while, she'd go to sword-training dojos to fight the students there, usually ten at a time, so she wouldn't lose her edge, and she always came back with bruises on her body. Whenever I tried to heal her with potions, she refused, saying it wasn't necessary for such minor wounds. But I'd feel guilty for Roland's sake if she ended up sustaining too many bruises and wounds. So, I made the effects more subtle.

And don't pick on people weaker than you too much, Francette.

…Don't come home with a signboard, okay?!

"Wh-What is that…?"

"You gotta have one of these in the hot springs. In my world, every hot spring has a lion at the spout. Yup!"

That wasn't true, of course. Besides, a lion would probably look out of place in Japanese hot springs.

"I-I see…"

Francette looked at it dubiously, but Belle and Layette were all over the lion head. The potion wouldn't affect their hands or anything just by touching the lion head, so I didn't stop them.

I also made it so the lion head would break and lose all of its effects if forcefully removed, just in case. Everything I made had a self-destruct mechanism, besides the single-use stuff. Even if it only had a mild effect, some influential or rich person could abuse it and cause a lot of trouble.

The women of the world would be greatly drawn to such an item, even if the effects were minute, so it was possible that one of them would make their influential husband or lover fight for it. How fearsome a woman's desire for beauty can be…

…Me? Give me kind-looking eyes, breasts, and more height! Damn it, I should have negotiated with Celes better…

No, I was going to fight fair and square with this appearance and with the genes I'd been given by my parents! I wasn't gonna cheat with my potions! I'd play the hand I'd been dealt…

"Why are you making funny faces?"

I wasn't!!!

Anyway, us four girls started doing girl talk, but…

There was nothing to talk about! My age was equivalent to my history without a boyfriend. Belle and Emile were technically a couple, but they didn't seem any different from when they had been orphans together. Layette was out of the question. That left…

"Francette, how are things with Roland?"

"Huh? What do you mean?"

"Oh, you know, just wondering how far you've gone…"

"What? We've been with you this entire time, so we haven't gone anywhere else since we left Grua…"

"…"

Belle and I exchanged looks, then I sighed.

She's hopeless…

So, I soaked in the water until my fingertips got wrinkly, then put my clothes on and called the guys over.

"That was way too long!"

Oh, I guess it was…

"Whoa, what the heck is that?!"

They were surprised by the unfamiliar object.

"What kind of animal is that?"

Huh? They didn't know what a lion was? Maybe lions didn't exist in this world, or at least not around here…

Well, there was no TV or animal encyclopedia, so maybe that wasn't unusual. If there wasn't any TV to watch, weren't any books to read, or any zoos to visit, I probably wouldn't have had an opportunity to see a lion, either. Not like they had lion mascots or anything like that, either.

I just laid around the girls' tent, listening to them talk in awe.

* *

"You want us to visit your village?"

"Y-Yeah. It's really close, only about two hours away. It's a small village, but a nice place. There are freshly picked vegetables, yams, and we've even got dishes with deer and boar meat! They're all really good!"

Oooh, deer and boar meat! And yams! ...But why were they looking around with shifty eyes?

Well, I was gonna go anyway. In this world, a two-hour walk was considered "really close." Though, I had to say, I was having a hard time believing that children would invite three armed strangers from another land to their homes so readily. Rural villagers are far more insular and suspicious of outsiders than most city folk might think. Well, maybe that's biased on my end, but at least it was true in my own experience.

"Why did you accept their invitation? Wasn't it a bit suspicious?"

"It was pretty suspicious."

"It was…"

Afterward, when I told the boys, "I guess we can check it out, then," one of them stayed behind to be our guide, and the other two said they were returning to the village because they 'had something to do.' They were obviously heading back first to prepare something…

We still hadn't gotten a chance to enjoy the hot springs to the fullest, so we weren't leaving quite yet. The plan was to stay for two nights and three days before heading out. Even in Japan, a hot springs trip of only one night and two days meant that you'd arrive in the evening, have a meal, and soak in the water once, only to leave in the morning, which just left you tired from going there and back with no time to relax. If you're going to the hot springs, you're supposed to stay there for a while and spend your time in blissful leisure. Get into the hot springs, get out, repeat. And, occasionally, maybe walk around to check out the local tourist sites…

I wondered what the small village in the mountains had in store to entertain us.

A village of bandits that robbed travelers blind? A village of criminals that lived with the families of human traffickers? It wasn't like I went around doing good deeds and volunteer work as a hobby, but if they wanted us to visit, then so be it.

I would go, along with the Fearsome Einherjar, the Valiant Royal Brother, and the Self-Detonating Fanatic...

"So, you want to go, knowing full well how suspicious this is..." Francette gave me an exasperated look, but I didn't mind.

"Yup. It seems interesting. Besides, I'm not one to back down from a challenge."

"...I know."

"I know..."

Layette repeated after Francette and Belle, despite not knowing what they were talking about. What a cutie.

The boy who had stayed behind to be our guide had also gone to the men's tent with the other guys. So, we had this discussion with just the girls.

"If it's a bandit village, we're going to wipe them out. We'll try to catch them without killing anyone, but our safety is the main priority, so don't hesitate to kill or incapacitate anyone if you sense that you're in any danger. I can cure anyone as long as they're not dead, anyway."

nod, nod

"I'd like to save the children, if at all possible, but they may already be trained to think a certain way and be beyond help. If they try to kill us without showing any remorse, take them out. The lives of my friends are a million times more important to me than some bandit kid's. Think of it this way. Risking your life to save a criminal doesn't mean you're putting just your own life in danger, but you're also putting my valued servant's life in danger."

nod, nod

There, now they should understand.

Every life is equally precious? If there's some idiot who thinks some grimy old bandit's life is worth just as much as Layette's, bring them to me! I'll straighten them out with an hour-long lecture! The choice between saving either an evil-looking, violent bandit, or a beautiful little girl, isn't even a question.

What's that? What if the choice was between an evil-looking, entirely average citizen and a beautiful little bandit girl? Uh. Urggh...

W-Well, anyway!

"Which one should we prioritize in that case, Kaoru?"

"Yes, we need to make sure we would know what to do!"

Francette and Belle pressed on.

Uhh...

"I-In that case, you should figure it out yourself!"

"Hey, you avoided the question!"

"She did..."

Sh-Shut up!

And so, after enjoying the hot springs for two more nights, we packed up the tent a little before the second daytime bell (around three in the afternoon) and started moving toward the village. During our trip, our guide had eaten his fill of the meals I made, so he was full of energy. He had also started doing some post-meal exercise... or, rather, he was attempting martial arts. Roland and Francette found this amusing and gave him some pointers, which the boy took very seriously. Emile and Belle joined in, turning it into an impromptu martial arts class.

Eat, train, hot springs (with healing effects)... This cycle was repeated over and over again. It goes without saying that this was highly effective. Having made visible progress in such a short time, with the guidance of professionals, the boy was in high spirits as he guided us toward the village. It really didn't feel like they were bandits setting a trap. The other two boys that had gone ahead to the village had just seemed like normal kids, and I hadn't gotten the impression that they were criminal types...

Maybe I was just being overly cautious? Though, dying from being overly cautious sounded a lot better than dying from a lack of caution, so that was fine by me. It wasn't like I was inconveniencing anyone, anyway.

Two hours or so later, we arrived at a small village in the mountains.

Although it was just a village, its perimeter was surrounded by a wooden fence. No military force was going to invade all the way out here, so maybe it was a bandit village, after all...

"It's for the wild beasts and monsters," Francette told me, upon seeing the look on my face and sensing what was in my head.

Come to think of it, those structures just wouldn't be enough to stop human invaders. It wasn't an issue of durability, but a human could just slip through the openings or climb over the top, so it was likely there to stop beasts and monsters, which would likely rely solely on brute force rather than wits. The fencing was only around the residential area, which was lined with houses, and the fields could be seen outside. I figured the fences were designed to stop monsters that ate humans, rather than the small animals that ate the crops, and putting up enough fencing to cover everything wasn't efficient.

As we walked toward the entrance section of the fence, some people working in the fields just outside the fences came over and gathered around us.

"Ohh, it's not every day we get visitors. Welcome. Well, enjoy your stay!"

"O-Okay…"

Hmm…

Everyone welcomed us with pleasant smiles. They were hard at work in their fields, and none of them struck me as bad people. They just seemed like Villager A, Villager B, Villager C, etc. It seemed that I had been mistaken in assuming that this would be a village full of bandits. But something was still bothering me…

Normally, a village that was so far off from the main roads, with no regular visitors to speak of, should have been pretty wary of outsiders. Not to mention, three out of the six of us were armed with swords, two of *those* were wearing expensive-looking gear, and for all they knew, we could've been a bunch of lower-class nobles or knights in name only, here to make unreasonable demands and take advantage of their hospitality. We didn't seem like the kind of guests who'd be the most welcome…

Plus, this was a small village. I found it hard to believe that those boys, who should have returned two days ago, hadn't spread the news about us yet. Interesting news spread like wildfire in places like this, and we should've been the talk of the whole village…

But they were acting as if nothing had happened.

Hmm…

Well, I supposed that meant it was too early to let my guard down. I shot Roland and Francette a glance, and they gave me a faint nod in return. They were pros when it came to battle and intrigue, so that was expected of them. Unlike low-ranking soldiers, knights and royals were learned in the ways of subtlety and trickery.

Several villagers walked up to talk to us, and in the meantime, I saw two or three of them moving toward the entrance of the fence. I figured that they were heading off to let the others know about us. It seemed like they were just ordinary farmers, and had no intention of using force on us…

Well, I was sure there were people with other occupations among them, like hunters and woodcutters, but in any case, they didn't seem like a group of criminals. Still, there was something off about them that kept me from dismissing this as just a normal village. The way those two boys had left, while leaving one of their number behind, felt very unnatural to me. They should have all left or all stayed together as a group. Though, really, it would've been a huge deal if they hadn't returned at all for two whole days without alerting their families, so the latter was pretty unlikely.

But why would they leave a kid with a bunch of strangers they had just met, especially since those strangers were planning on staying for two more nights? And didn't they think the boy's family would freak out when they delivered that news? Not to mention, the boy's family had never come to meet up with the boy over these past two days, despite being a mere two-hour walk away.

…Well, I supposed that answered my question.

Chapter 35: Siege

"Ah, it must have been quite a trip for you, coming all the way out here in the mountains! Welcome! I am Hasdal, the village mayor. Please, stay the night in my humble home."

There was no way that there would ever be an inn at a village like this. The mayor's house was bigger than the rest in small villages, mainly for the purpose of housing and feeding travelers and visitors. So, declining his offer wasn't really an option. It wasn't like we couldn't camp outside, but turning him down would be discourteous and would make the mayor lose face.

But this did make me wonder... There was a very obvious question he should have asked us in the beginning. That being, "What is the purpose of your visit?"

Though, he probably didn't ask, because he already knew that those boys had brought us here...

Anyway, our guide thanked us for the meals and the martial arts lessons, then ran off to his own house as we made our way to the mayor's house.

"Urgh!"

We entered the mayor's house and got led into the main hall to find a large group of men sitting there. The youngest ones seemed to be fifteen to sixteen years old, having just recently come of age, and the oldest ones looked to be about sixty...

Unlike in modern Japan, sixty-year-olds in this world were pretty much ancient. Maybe it was their diet, or the harsh living conditions…

"The meal will be ready soon, so please relax here with the others…" With that, the mayor went toward the back of the building, presumably into the kitchen.

"W-Wait a minute…" I whispered quietly, and Francette replied in a hushed voice, "D-Don't tell me…"

"A marriage hunting party for single villagers who can't find a wife!"

"No, it's not!!!"

The men all shouted at once, in response to the comment that Francette and I had yelled without thinking.

They didn't have to deny it that *vigorously…*

"Besides, all that's left on your side is a kid and an infant!"

Sh-Shut up!

The mayor returned, the food was brought out, and it was time for us to all dine together. There weren't really any deep conversations going on during the meal, and the villagers mainly seemed to talk about whatever nonsense came to mind. As such, we opted to stick to normal girl talk (that wasn't very girly) that we were okay with the others overhearing. Roland and Emile were busy muttering things to each other. The food came on large plates, in the style of a big feast, but the ingredients were run-of-the-mill crops and boar meat, which had presumably been procured by the hunters.

They weren't just feeding us, but a mass of villagers as well, so they couldn't get too extravagant. The villagers seemed to understand this, as well. There seemed to be a lot of food at first glance, but it was a relatively small amount when considering the number of people there, so they only scooped small portions onto their plates, so as to not make it seem like there wasn't enough food.

Why did they go through so much trouble to gather all these people here, I wonder...

*   *

The not-so-extravagant meal ended quickly. There was actually more food portioned out on the plates near us, and the villagers didn't try to touch those. Feeling a bit suspicious, I extended the range of the poison-detecting bracelet's effects, but found nothing out of the ordinary.

Now that the meal was done, I figured it was time to bring up the main topic.

Maybe they were planning on making us repay them for the meal and lodging? Drifting gamblers relying on the hospitality of their local gaming parlor owner might have had such an obligation, but we were invited here.

What's going to happen now...?

"Well then, it's time to begin our monthly village meeting. Our guests may only be here on the day of our meeting by coincidence, but since they *are* currently present, they are free to give their input, just like our fellow villagers, without any reservations. We could learn much from a fresh perspective, after all. Hohoho!"

Lies!!! Like hell it's a coincidence! They timed everything so we'd be here on this day on purpose!

Roland, Francette, Emile and Belle stared at the mayor with accusatory eyes. But it seemed that he hadn't made it to his position as the mayor without developing the appropriate skills. He was completely unconcerned by the cold looks that all of us (excluding Layette) were giving him.

The meeting went on, and we were sometimes asked questions like, "What sort of crops are selling in the cities?" and "What kinds of crafted products are the prosperous villages selling?"

"Now, on to the final topic. How to deal with the bandits and their demand for a 'protection fee,' in the form of valuables, food, and women. Any ideas?"

There it is!!! Let's see how everyone else is reacting...

Yup, Layette looked like she wasn't thinking about anything at all.

So cute...

Likewise, Emile and Belle had blank looks on their own faces.

It wasn't that they'd given up on thinking. If anything happened, after all, they would just follow me and do whatever I said... Wait, they *had* given up on thinking!

Roland wore an awkward expression. In his mind, the royal family had a duty to protect its people. But this wasn't his kingdom, and the duty to protect these people fell to the nobles and royals of their nation, not to him. Besides, the royal family was supposed to protect their subjects through administration, not by swinging the sword themselves. But, as a member of the royal line—no, as a man—could he really abandon people in trouble right before his eyes? That's probably what was going through his head...

As for Francette...

There was a twinkle in her eyes. They were sparkling like crazy!

A traveling knight arrives at a village in danger. The knight cuts down the mob of villains, and as she turns to leave, a voice can be heard from behind...

"Please, what is your name...?"

"I am Francette. An einherjar of no consequence..."

I could tell that kind of scene was being played out, in her head, right that moment.

...She's hopeless!

A man with noble features and expensive equipment, who was clearly an aristocrat traveling incognito... A young woman, who seemed to be his wife or lover, also in expensive-looking equipment... Two hunters, likely brother and sister, or even lovers, who appeared to have been hired as bodyguards... A maid, accompanying them to handle the two nobles' needs... And, finally, a little commoner girl, who they had presumably taken into their care along the way.

Yeah, from an outsider's perspective, they were obviously a noble couple with a soft spot for commoners on a sight-seeing trip. Moreover, the nobleman clearly sympathized with the village's plight, and his wife/lover was exuding an aura of enthusiasm. In fact, it was gushing out of every pore of her body like a geyser. I could tell the mayor was desperately trying to stifle a grin upon seeing all of this.

Well, I supposed that was to be expected, considering that he thought the decision-maker of the group was at least partially on board, and the woman, who he presumed to be the actual highest authority due to her influence over said decision-maker, was fully ready to help. It was uncommon for noblemen to simply ignore a woman's request, after all. Especially if it was from the woman they were romantically involved with.

And the opinions of the bodyguards, maid, and the little girl... they were irrelevant.

...Or so he thinks.

The mayor and villagers looked at us... or, rather, at Roland and Francette, expectantly.

191

Then, unable to withstand the pressure, Francette finally said, "You can count on us—"

Not so fast!

"…To pray for the safety of your village, so please don't hesitate to ask your liege lord for assistance!"

Francette began to make a careless comment, but I cut her off immediately.

"Whaaaaaat?!"

The kind and simple-looking noblewoman was just about to give the reply they were all waiting for, and just as they were reveling in their victory, an unexpected interruption had ruined it all. The looks on the villagers' faces went from confusion to anger.

Well, I suppose that's natural…

"Know your place, maid! Keep your mouth shut and do as your master says!"

"Yeah, that's…"

Then, the mood suddenly got tense.

"Huh…?"

Just as the mayor raised his voice in anger at me, and the other villagers followed suit…

Well, first, the air grew cold.

Francette, whose eyes had been sparkling just a moment ago…

Roland, who had been mulling over the idea…

Emile and Belle, who were entirely unconcerned until then, leaving the decision completely up to me…

And even Layette, who was just sitting there absentmindedly…

They all glared back at the mayor and villagers with fury in their eyes.

"I am impressed, Kaoru. You saw through to their true nature: lowly and unworthy of saving."

192

"I am disgusted. We're leaving. I refuse to defile myself by staying in this village a moment longer!"

"...Can we destroy this place before we leave?"

The villagers and their mayor went white in the face. It seemed that they had quickly realized the mistake that they had made.

Hey, don't look at me with those pleading eyes. I'm just the maid, after all.

*   *

"Please forgive uuuuus!!!"

The village mayor rubbed his head against the floor in apology, the other villagers in a similar position behind him.

After that unfortunate incident, the mayor had thrown out all his schemes and bargaining tactics and finally spat out the truth. According to him, the situation was as follows:

They were a small village: not particularly wealthy, but able to lead a modest life, sustaining their needs with agriculture, forestry, hunting, gathering, and the occasional trip to the nearby hot springs for their leisure.

Then, one day, *they* arrived. The aforementioned bandits. But instead of attacking and robbing the villagers, they brought a proposition with them:

"We'll protect your village, so give us your valuables, food, and women as compensation."

What a joke.

Apparently, they thought to prey on this village to supplement their less-than-stable thieving business. Instead of robbing them blind in one fell swoop, they wanted a steady supply of food and revenue. And a steady supply of women. They were also planning to use the village to recruit new underlings.

Though, under that plan, they would run out of young women and girls, and once they expended all the young adults and boys of the village as human shields and disposable grunts, the village would only be left with senior citizens.

But that wasn't a big deal. If that happened, they would take what was left of the village and move on to the next place. The troubling part was, they had acted as if they were proposing a legitimate protection service. Due to this fake posturing, the village couldn't seek help from their lord. There hadn't been any harm done yet, and these bandits were technically just "proposing a protection contract." They were merely offering up the conditions of the contract, and they weren't making threats or committing any crimes in the process, though no one knew what would happen if the villagers actually refused.

It would have helped if they'd had proof that these bandits had engaged in previous acts of banditry, but there was no way to tell who their past victims had been, and it wasn't as if there were any local merchants, much less any who had survived their attacks. Even if there had been, they would likely have been far too busy running for their lives to remember the faces of their attackers. Besides, the bandits could simply deny any such claims, and there wouldn't be anything that could be done about it.

And even if their lord sent out soldiers to help, the bandits could just rob people in some other region, then return once the soldiers left. It was unrealistic to expect the soldiers to stay in a distant village like this one over a long period of time. Besides, sending soldiers to some tiny village in the mountains to fight bandits, risking casualties in the process, was far more costly than simply letting the villagers get sucked dry. The lord could just ignore the issue and keep collecting levies without bothering to decrease taxes. It wouldn't be surprising if he came to such a conclusion, honestly. Although, this may have been different if the village in question paid higher taxes, or produced rare materials…

"…So, instead of doing something about it yourselves, you wanted to trick a bunch of unrelated foreigners from another country into fighting the bandits for you? Even though there are children among us, and only three of us are even capable of fighting?"

The villagers likely assumed from Belle's appearance that she was a fighter, but her dagger was basically just for intimidation. At best, she could only take down one person with her. Belle's self-proclaimed role was to be my shield and buy a few seconds until Emile or Francette could rush to my side. She would cling on to the sword that impaled her so the attacker couldn't retrieve it…

Wait, like hell I'd let her do that!

"N-No! We did not expect your small group to fight off nearly thirty bandits alone!"

Well, we could, but… yeah. Pretty easily, too.

"We will fight too, of course! Gathered here today are the men of the village, minus the children and young men without offspring. However, although we are hardy from rigorous labor, we are all amateurs when it comes to fighting men. The only ones who have some basic ability in a fight would be the hunters, but their expertise is in fighting beasts, and will not be of much use in this case."

But even as he spoke, the mayor's eyes had vigor in them.

"A young man going to the city to make his name in the world is one thing, but if families with elderly parents and young children abandoned this village to move to the city, they couldn't survive with just their skills in farming, logging, and hunting. The best they could hope for would be to rot away in the slums. In that case, we may as well risk it all in a fight... Even if we fall in battle, it would be a thousand times better than running away without a fight and watching our loved ones starve to death! So, when the children informed us that some travelers had arrived, travelers who seemed to have fighting experience at that, we couldn't help ourselves. We want all the help we can get. We want to raise our chances of winning, no matter how small they might be. And we will give up our lives if we can increase our chances of saving the women and children, even if we end up in hell rather than heaven..."

With that, the mayor pressed his head against the ground once more. Looking again, I realized that quite a few of the people here were advanced in their years. Instead of being protected, the elderly were going to sacrifice themselves to help the younger generation live just a little longer. That even included the mayor himself...

Hmm, I see.

I see...

I stood up, arms folded, then said, "Mayor. Why did you use such schemes to try to drag us into this?"

"..." The mayor kept his head down, unable to respond.

So, I continued.

"Instead of plotting, you should have said: 'We are going to put our lives on the line to fight for our village. Please help us.' That was all you needed to do..."

The mayor and villagers kept their heads down...

*   *

"That was incredible, Kaoru!" Francette said as soon as the villagers left and it was just our group in the room that we were assigned to. Roland and Layette followed.

"Indeed."

"Incredoru?"

Francette grew ecstatic any time I did Goddess-like things that encouraged people to have faith in me. Roland also seemed glad to be able to participate in protecting the populace. Emile and Belle's reactions... went without saying.

And Layette, what the heck was "Incredoru"? Had she combined "Incredible" and "Kaoru"?!

Anyway, this wasn't a task suitable for my main role as the owner of Convenience Store Belle, but rather something for the Eyes of the Goddess. Though, it wasn't like I was obligated to do anything. I suppose this was like a club activity I did as a hobby.

Man, I'm too easy...

"All right, our staff vacation is put on hold, as of right now. From here on, we're going to set aside common sense and move forward as the Eyes of the Goddess..."

nod, nod, nod, nod

Okay, let's gooo!

Earlier, we'd had a conversation with the villagers. They had been driven out of their original lands due to circumstances beyond their control long ago and hadn't had any choice but to develop a village deep in the mountains. They'd lost many of their companions along the way, and they weren't going to just let all the hard work of their ancestors go to waste because some lowly bandits said so.

And they claimed they didn't mind if most of the men gathered here died, as long as they could protect the village itself. As long as the women, children, and young adults lived, the village would survive and their knowledge would be passed on. Then, the next generation could have many children. That way, their lives, too, would be passed on.

"Our deaths will not be in vain."

Rather than abandon their village and flee, only to end up in the gutter of some slum and perish, full of regrets, they would die with pride and with their heads held high...

As the mayor and the others said so with a laugh, they no longer had a subservient air about them.

Maybe they've gotten over it...

In any case, it was time to prepare for battle.

"So, I will dive into the enemy's ranks and take out about half of them right at the start. I'm sure Sir Roland and Emile also wish to succeed in front of Kaoru, so we can split the remainder evenly among the three of us..."

It seemed that Emile wanted to shoot down this idea, but he also knew that he wouldn't be able to take on an even third of the entire enemy force. Realizing this, he seemed a bit reluctant, but nodded without saying another word.

As for Roland, he was accustomed to thinking that he didn't have to directly defeat enemies, but that using his subordinates to achieve victory would add to his own glory, so he didn't seem to mind.

But...

"That's no good. We can't just produce a deus ex machina and conveniently solve all their problems without the villagers lifting a finger. They wouldn't learn anything or grow from this at all. What do they do if they face another danger when we're not here? What about after that? And after that?"

"Urgh..." Francette couldn't respond.

"And what do you think will happen if word of this spreads? Everyone will think they can just wait for a savior when facing their own dangers. They'll think, 'Someone will come and save us, just like that village!' They need to overcome obstacles with their own hands. Getting a little help is one thing, but relying entirely on God or other people doesn't do anyone any good. Besides, that's not what they want."

Francette looked down wordlessly, seemingly ashamed of her own imprudence.

Surprisingly, Emile responded, "That's because everyone doesn't know about Kaoru's power, or our own. If they did, they would have asked for our help differently. Besides, would you be okay with letting people get hurt or die when we have the power to save them?"

"Yeah."

"...Huh?" Emile seemed surprised by my reply.

But that's just the way of the world. You can't just rely on everyone else for everything while taking on zero risk yourself. If that became the norm, humans would go real rotten real quick.

Roland and Francette seemed to understand. Wisdom comes with age, I suppose. Francette was over thirty now, come to think of it.

No, the villagers wouldn't be dying this time. I'd make them fight for themselves, but we'd be helping a bit.

Yes, just a bit...

*   *

"Heh heh, well? Have you decided to take us up on our offer yet? It's not like you have a choice, after all, so just hurry up and accept it. All you gotta do is give us all your money, feed us as much as we like, and send some women our way to take care of some chores. That's a pretty good deal for protecting a whole village, if you ask me."

With that, the three men sent by the bandit group laughed vulgarly.

"...Hm?"

One of them had a perplexed look on his face.

"What the hell are you giving us that look for?!"

The last time they'd visited, with their leader present, the villagers had had a much more fearful, nearly subservient attitude. But this time, there was defiance in their eyes.

"You think you can act up because it's just the three of us?! Listen here, we're from the famous bandit group, the Beasts of Disaster..."

"And?"

"Huh?"

Something was off. Very off. The three men finally came to this realization.

After being shown to the mayor's house, they had given what was basically an ultimatum to the mayor and the several elderly men gathered there. They had planned on making the villagers accept all of their terms, maybe taking a few young women with them, and stopping somewhere nearby to relieve them of their virginity. So, they had struggled to win their highly-coveted positions as the members who would come on this excursion. All they had to do now was reap the benefits of their role. Or so they thought...

"Here is our response."

The mayor opened his mouth.

"We refuse your proposal. What we would need to give up for what little benefit you've offered is far from acceptable. That is, the money, food, and... young girls... you've demanded. And, above all, we do not trust you in the least. No one in our village is stupid enough to make such an agreement with a group that's so unlikely to keep a promise..."

The bandits watched, mouths agape, as the mayor went on matter-of-factly. Then, as the words finally began sinking in...

"Wha?! What the hell is this? You know what'll happen if you don't do as we..."

"I wonder...?"

"Y-You little... I'll kill you and make an example out of ya! The rest of the village will see we mean business if we kill a couple..."

"All right, there's an admission that you're a bunch of bandits, along with a declaration of your intent to murder, as well as intimidation, and even assault by grabbing an elderly man's collar. This fulfills the conditions for self-defense and is reason enough to defeat the bandits!" yelled Kaoru.

"Wha..."

Five men and women suddenly appeared from the room next door. Their clothing and features made it clear they weren't from the village.

"You bastards the ones who put these geezers up to this?! I'll kill you first... Gwah!"

Bam! Smack!

As the bandits were distracted by Kaoru's speech, Francette, Roland, and Emile had snuck up behind them. And unlike Roland, Francette and Emile wouldn't sit idly by and allow some lowly bandits to talk down to or threaten Kaoru.

The three bandits fell to the ground. As for Belle, she stood in front of Kaoru in a low posture, her hands crossed over her chest.

"Good! You're fulfilling your role well, Belle. You must use your body as a shield for Lady Kaoru at all times!"

Upon hearing Francette's words, Kaoru snapped.

"It was youuuuuu! I was wondering why I could never stop Belle from being so self-sacrificing, but it was all your doinggg!!!"

*   *

We took out three of them for now. When the bandit leader and his men had first arrived, the villagers counted twenty-nine men. … Which left twenty-six more.

I treated the three we had captured with healing potions just enough so that they wouldn't die, had them tied up, then gave them some medicine that would lower their metabolic speed. They wouldn't be capable of joining any fights until they were given a neutralizing agent first.

Francette and the others captured these three, but that wasn't a big deal. Even if we weren't around, the villagers could have easily defeated them by ambushing them with bamboo spears or putting poison in the food or water. So, by the time they had gotten around to fighting back against the bandits, they were guaranteed to at least take out three of the enemy.

It just so happened that the enraged Francette and the others beat them first, and taking out the messengers was only the first step of the villagers' plans.

"Lady Kaoru, we've finished reinforcing the palisade. Please take a look."

"Ah, all right."

One of the villagers reported to me, so I stood up in response. Francette and the others followed, of course. Once the fight against the bandits had been agreed to, I had given several orders to the villagers. One of them being, naturally, the reinforcement of the palisade around the village.

The palisade was built for keeping out monsters, and it was far too fragile and the gaps in it too large to be of any use against human attackers. As such, I had it modified and reinforced as a countermeasure against the bandits.

"Yeah, that's pretty good. Definitely a passing mark. Now, about the water buckets…"

The villagers looked thrilled to win my seal of approval, then quickly ran off to carry the water buckets.

This palisade was a defensive structure, originally designed to stop charging orcs and ogres while spears were held out between the openings. Therefore, it didn't account for smaller monsters like goblins, kobolds, and horn rabbits. And, of course, humans.

It had been modified by narrowing the gaps between the stretches of palisade and installing sharp stakes on the open edges to cut up anyone who tried to force their way between them. The parts that had wider gaps intentionally left open had such traps built into them with extra attention.

Of course, poison would be applied to them before the actual showdown. This village had hunters, and unlicensed apothecaries too, so they could prepare poison extracted from plants and poisonous monsters without my interference.

As everyone checked the status of the fences, several of the villagers came over with buckets of water.

Time to pretend to reach into my pocket and make some potions!

I produced some convenient medicine inside a test tube…

"Good work. Please leave it there."

The villagers placed the buckets on the ground, and I dropped a few drops of the potion into each one.

"Slowly pour this water on the ground under the palisade and around the stakes. Apply it to the palisade and the spikes, as well. It will make the wood more durable. If you run out of water, refill the buckets and call for me. I will add more of the medicine."

This should have been an acceptable amount of help. I was just making the palisade a little stronger, and if they had taken the time, they could have reinforced the palisade themselves, even without my potions. I was just using items to reduce the required time. Just like spending money on in-app purchases. It wasn't cheating.

I decided to check the effects of the durability-enhancing water, which I had dubbed the "Super Hard Liquid Coating." The effects should be instantaneous, so I should have been able to check the effects immediately after application.

I first pulled on a stake that secured the fence to the ground... and it didn't move. It didn't budge one bit.

"Fran, can you test the durability of the stakes?"

Maybe Francette's powerful arms would have better luck than my noodle arms?

"...A powerful foe."

Francette tried to pull the fence out, but only managed to move the stake and the ground around it very slightly. It seemed to be far from being pulled free. The stake itself didn't seem to be breakable, either...

Judging by the look of it, it may have been possible to slip through between the palisade sections, but breaking the palisade itself seemed highly unlikely. And if someone did squeeze through, the sharp stakes and thorns would cause a lot of damage to any poor sap who tried. Besides, they were coated in poison.

"Kaoru, what should we call this medicine, or I should say, the palisade coated in this medicine?" Francette asked. She was probably asking to note it in that "Records of the Goddess Kaoru's World Reformation" diary that she secretly kept, all without realizing that I knew all about it.

Well, not like I minded. She could keep a diary if she wanted.

...But I wouldn't let her publish it! But I didn't think to name it...

Hmm...

When you knock on it with your hand, it feels and sounds rigid.

And when you pour the medicine on it, it erases time and only leaves the result, like King Crimson.

You go "kon" with your hand (te), and it becomes King Crimson...

Te goes kon, into kincri...

Tekkon, kincree...

"Tekkonkinkreet, a.k.a. Tekkon!"

Yes, the Nagase Clan's horrible naming sensibilities were still alive and well...

*   *

"...Bring me the village mayor."

Two bandits had come to visit. This time, they stayed outside of the entrance of the fence and made their demands from there. They must have found it suspicious that the three men they had sent previously hadn't returned yet.

...Well, they'd have been idiots if they hadn't.

Francette and I were hiding in the shack near the entrance, listening to their exchange. This shack was where the people on night watch duty took turns resting during periods of danger, like when monsters came to attack. The only furnishings were a couple of chairs and a table that looked like reused junk, but it was better than nothing.

The young men who had responded to the bandits yelling at the entrance called the mayor over.

"Yes, how can I help you...?"

The mayor was a pretty good actor. Must have been the wisdom that came with age.

"Our men should have come by yesterday! Where are they?!"

Yep, of course they came to check. And the mayor's reply...

"Indeed, the three of them did pay us a visit."

"Well? Where are they?!"

The bandits aren't in a very good mood. That was to be expected, I suppose...

"Oh? They left right after. They said they were acting on their leader's orders, and we gave them all the money we had, plenty of non-perishable food, water in a leather bag, and three of the best-looking young girls in the village..."

"Huh?"

The two bandits seemed dumbfounded. Then, the mayor's words finally seemed to sink in.

"Wh-What?!"

"We only did as we were told by your messengers... Their words were their leader's words, or that's what we've been told..."

The bandits look troubled! What will they do now...?

"...Damn it! We'll be back!"

Ah, they'd retreated to get new orders from their leader. Not like they had any other option, really.

They thought their men had betrayed them and ran off with the money, food, and girls. They couldn't let the villagers realize this, or they'd expose their lack of solidarity and make themselves look bad. Of course they'd try to hide that. And, to make sure others didn't follow suit, they had to catch and make an example out of the deserters. Now, they'd waste days trying to punish traitors who didn't exist. During that time, we would continue our preparations.

The reason we hadn't made a move on the visitors today was, of course, because we thought they might have suspected their previous messengers could have been attacked, and may even have stationed other bandits to keep watch on us from afar. That, or they could have already suspected the previous messengers had betrayed them, and had someone keeping watch on their own men. Either way, it was too dangerous to make a move this time. That was all.

"All right, let's keep working, then!"

"Yeeeah!!!" the villagers all shouted at once.

The village was becoming much more cheerful. But they were still just doing as they were told, and all their work was without risk, so far. When it came down to it, would they be able to break out of their shells as herbivores? Could they stand up to their carnivorous oppressors?

Would they flee, or would they give up their own lives to deliver a sting, like the honeybee does? I remembered a manga I had bought at a used book store long ago. In that story, all the old people had willingly stayed to shoot at their enemies, buying time for the younger generation to get on a ship and fly off to space...

Did the old people of this village have that same resolve? A famous line from a certain title came to mind. *"Why do you think tigers are strong? Because they're strong by nature!"* Tigers don't lift weights or train to learn special moves. But they're strong. That's because they were born as tigers.

But the bandits were no tigers. They were nothing but stray dogs, trying to make themselves look big with weapons and violence. These men lacked the talent to become hunters, the discipline to become soldiers, the diligence to become merchants, the skills to become craftsmen, and the endurance to become farmers. What would be exposed from under their bravado when their desperate attempt at intimidation failed and the villagers they looked down on retaliated...?

*   *

A few days later, the villagers had already formed their rural village defense organization, Arc Path.

Farming was an occupation that cultivated life through the creation of crops. A farmer who planned to kill other people was a farmer who had lost their way. But, this time, they had no choice. So, they hadn't completely fallen off of their path, but it was more like they had deviated from it in an arc, which was how they had gotten their name.

…I named them, of course.

What? I thought it sounded cool!

There had been a lot of progress on the upgrades for the palisade since the first messengers had arrived. Using the extra time we had bought, the palisade had been completely reinforced. We had even set various traps around it and in the surrounding woods, as well as the bushes where the bandits might set up camp.

The traps ranged from highly advanced ones to cheap tricks. Some of them were literally made by the village kids, and might not even trigger properly. But with there being deadly traps in the mix, the bandits had to deal with each one as if it was highly dangerous. This restricted their actions and narrowed their range of options. And so…

"They're here!"

The lookout alerted us as Francette and I were waiting at the shack on standby. From there, we could hear any conversations at the entrance. Roland and Emile were at a nearby house, while Belle and Layette were waiting in a house further away.

After some time, two bandits appeared. They called for the mayor like last time, to talk… or, rather, to intimidate the villagers.

"Heh, we're back. Now, I'll need you to give us money, food, and women, like we mentioned…"

It seemed they had given up on finding the "traitors that had run away."

"What? We already gave you all of our money, food, and young girls. What are you talking about?"

"Urgh… Whatever. That's not important, damn it!"

Unable to come up with a retort, the bandit yelled and tried to cover it up. But the mayor didn't let up.

"You claim not to have received what we have already given you, and now you demand more? What kind of agreement is this?! Besides, are you truly even the same bandits who came here last time? I find it suspicious that you claim you haven't gotten what we've handed over already! The person we gave everything to was definitely from the same group as the first visit. Some of us remember their faces. But we don't recognize any of you…"

"Wh-What are you…"

They didn't want us to know that they allegedly had a traitor. And even if they confessed, that wouldn't be reason enough for the villagers to want to pay them again. That left the bandits with limited options.

The conversation came to a deadlock and the bandits seemed rather troubled, but then the mayor brought up a suggestion.

"If someone who we recognize…not the leader, but someone who's distinct enough that they stood out, like that bald man with a wound on his cheek…and that silver-haired man who looked a bit frail to be a bandit… If those two were here, we would know that they were definitely messengers from your leader. Then we would be open for negotiations…"

The two messengers cursed at the mayor, then left. Their next visit would be when we made our move.

*   *

"I'm the boss's second, Deyles, and this here's Exdel, his advisor. We're here, just like you wanted! Now, you'd better…"

The baldy and the slender guy had come with two others, making a total of four bandits. The mayor and villagers waited some distance away from the entrance, further inside the palisade, so the bandits moved forward and took a few steps toward them. Then…

"Wha…"

The entrance suddenly slammed shut, and several villagers sprang out of hiding and charged, each of them gripping a bamboo spear in their hands.

"Y-You bastards!"

Wham! Wham!

The bamboo spears were thrust into each of the bandits in quick succession. The bandits were definitely not masters of the sword, and there was no way that they could have parried so many attacks at once.

In a desperate battle between amateurs with no experience in martial arts, the difference in fighting abilities tends to be rather insignificant. And in cases where there was just a slight difference in power, that disadvantage could be overcome with superior reach and numbers. The four bandits couldn't do anything against an ambush with so many long bamboo spears coming at them all at once.

Why had the villagers gone through so much trouble to set this up instead of just killing the messengers last time? Since they only had one chance to conduct an ambush, it was obviously better to use that chance to its maximum possible effect. That was why we had baited out the highest priority targets available.

Since the bandit leader was unlikely to come himself, they wanted to take out the second-in-command and the advisor, the latter of whom was the reason that the bandits were able to maneuver relatively well in the first place. According to the three bandits the villagers had captured, those two were the brains of the operation. The leader may have been strong and charismatic but, apparently, he had muscles for brains...

Now, the bandit group had fallen from being formidable and cunning foes into just another pack of meatheads. Not only that, but the bandits would be blind with rage from losing their key members. When they did invade, they'd meet a counterattack carried out by Roland, Francette, myself, and the members of Arc Path, who had been taught how to fight without mercy. The preparations to defeat the bandits were complete!

But Roland and Francette...

I didn't know you two were capable of torture and teaching people how to fight dirty...

I didn't think knights and royals did that kind of stuff.

"They'll probably come first thing tomorrow morning..."

Once they got the shocking news, it would be like a bolt from the blue, and they'd be left dumbfounded for some time, then go wild with rage. It would be near sundown by the time they made preparations and mobilized, so they'd probably come early tomorrow morning.

Well, that was assuming there was someone watching from afar who reported the incident right away, but judging by how no one had come to see what was happening after their second had been gone for so long, they were likely aware of what was going on.

In any case, I decided I would try to get some sleep tonight. Some of the villagers were standing watch in case the bandits tried to sneak in and take the girls and children hostage. And, of course, we weren't part of the guard duty rotation. So, we would rest up for tomorrow.

*   *

The next morning arrived.

It went without saying that I had woken up early, had some food, and washed my face in preparation for the bandits. Though it went against their usual routine, I had instructed the villagers to each have a light meal, too. It would've been bad if they were to get stabbed in the stomach when it was full, but I figured it would be worse if things went south when they still hadn't eaten since last night, causing them to run out of energy.

Well, I did have potions for if they got stabbed in the stomach.

And so, their group arrived. There were about twenty of them, so it was probably everyone they had left. Twenty-nine minus three minus four makes twenty-two. ...Yeah, it was right around that number.

Francette and I were hiding in the nearby shack again.

The bandits stopped at a spot some distance away, far enough that even arrows wouldn't reach, then sent a grunt over to the closed gate. The runner stopped in front of the gate.

"Bring out your mayor! Your..."

Wham!

"Huh...?" He looked rather confused for a moment, then looked down at the "feathered accessory" sprouting from his chest with a surprised expression, then fell to the floor, never to rise again.

The hunters shot rabbits and birds on a regular basis. There was no way they would miss a stationary target from such a short distance.

Twenty-one left.

"You bastaaards!!!"

The one shouting seemed to be their leader.

Shooting down their runner without hearing him out meant that the villagers denied them completely... in fact, it was a declaration of war. They had no intention of talking, now. Well, that should have been clear from the way the villagers had taken out their second-in-command last time, but they had decided to try to talk it out anyway, and ended up letting another one of their men die for nothing.

Rest in peace...

We do not negotiate with criminals and terrorists. Bargaining and tricking the opponent are all fine, though. No need to diligently follow the rules when your opponents clearly don't. We should use all the trickery and traps we've got, instead.

Oh, and we hadn't killed the three bandits that had come by earlier. Once we tied them up and gave them a weakening potion, there was no risk of them helping the enemy side, even if they managed to get rescued. Unlike muscle relaxants, weakening potions were safe to take, so no worries there. If you were to drink it, it would just render you unable to move your limbs, without affecting your breathing, heart, or other organs. And even if those bandits we captured did get away, they were just some peons, so they wouldn't have made much of a difference.

But that wasn't the case for the second-in-command. If he had escaped, it would've been a big blow to us. Nothing's harder to deal with than a cunning villain. Also, I had to give the villagers some confidence before the main battle. They had to see for themselves that, while bandits may act tough, they were really nothing to fear.

Yes, bandits are weak. Not once have I seen or heard of bandits who spent every day training in martial arts. Though, I guess it's possible that a few such bandits exist...

In any case, the majority of bandits haven't received real training in any official capacity, and didn't practice to improve themselves each day. They were merely ordinary men who were feared because they flashed weapons at defenseless, unarmed people, and were prepared to use violence on harmless folk. In fact, farmers, miners, hunters, and woodcutters could beat them easily in a straight-up fight.

Besides, if they really were strong, they would have gotten into an actual, legitimate profession and become hunters, mercenaries, contract bodyguards, or other security personnel. They wouldn't have been here, debasing themselves by being bandits.

So, what would happen if the villagers all came at them with the intent to kill, without holding back and without regard for their own lives? We intended to show the bandits just that.

"Get 'em, men!"

Wham!

An arrow landed on another bandit, but it hit a reinforced part of his armor, so it was unfortunately rather ineffective. The bandits arrived at the gate before the next arrow was fired, but when they tried to open it...

Slam!

"Gyaaaaaa!"

Bam! Thud! Fwip!

The gate wasn't just a board, but another obstacle, with open slits like the rest of the palisade. It was made so it could be moved from the side to block the gate section, and bamboo spears could be thrust out from the spaces around the gate.

Two bandits carelessly approached the gate to move it to the side and open it, and spears were thrust into them. The villagers holding the spears had been hiding until it was their time to strike.

Even the bandits wouldn't have been dumb enough to heedlessly walk up to villagers holding spears out in front of them.

…Now there were nineteen left.

"D-Damn it! Forget the gate, attack from all sides!"

Most of the bandits were equipped with swords. Maybe they thought swords were cooler, or that swords were somehow better for bandits, or that long spears got in the way when moving through the forest. Regardless, none of them were holding a spear, for whatever reason. They didn't have any bows, either. Maybe arrows were hard to come by for bandits, or bladed weapons were better for intimidating villagers, or it was harder to look tough with a bow when arguments broke out…

Anyway, they seemed to realize that they were at a disadvantage fighting over the palisade and the gate without any spears or bows, so they decided to prioritize getting past the undefended sections. They had observed during their last visit that the structures were designed in such a way that regular people could easily get through them. It seemed that the bandit leader wasn't the boss for nothing, as he wasted no time in giving out orders, despite having lost his second.

The time for direct confrontation had finally come. The villagers grew tense, but they were past the point of getting cold feet, and they stood tall with bamboo spears and their familiar farming tools in hand. Those who were in hiding had revealed themselves, and everyone, including me and Francette, was now out in the open. Though, the bandits wouldn't care about some unarmed girl.

…Except maybe to take as a hostage, anyway. But it was unlikely that they would be taking hostages at this point.

If word got out that they'd needed to take hostages from a bunch of villagers, they'd be done for. No one would be afraid of a gang of bandits with such a terrible reputation. They could still go for it, if they got desperate enough, but with Francette being right next to me, I wasn't really worried. Besides, once the fighting really kicked into gear, Roland and Emile would come flying out of hiding. I had ordered Belle to protect Layette, who was hiding in a house in the center of the village. Not in the mayor's residence, which the bandits might try to take over, but in an ordinary house.

Belle had insisted she wanted to guard me, but I used my special move, *"I give you my divine order to protect Layette,"* and she did as she was told. As for the current state of the battle...

"Agh!"

"Urgh, damn!"

"Ahhh!"

The bandits screamed in pain whenever they tried to slip in between the palisade sections and consequently got shredded by the spikes placed there. And, once their movement was impaired, they were quickly impaled with bamboo spears. The bandits who managed to get through tried to hurry away before the spear-wielding villagers came for them, but they were typically bleeding all over with pretty deep wounds.

"Huh...?"

And, of course, the spikes were coated in poison.

Just in case there had been any accidents, I decided not to use poison that could cause instant death or anything. I didn't want the villagers to accidentally prick themselves and end up dying. As long as they were still alive, I could use a healing potion, or rather, the Tears of the Goddess, to cure them. I had gone with this approach for safety purposes, but if they ended up being attacked by bandits again when I wasn't around, they would likely have to use a quicker-acting, deadlier poison. Obviously.

And so, a total of fourteen bandits made it past the palisade, half of them looking pale from the poison spikes and the other half having somehow managed to avoid getting stabbed, with nearly thirty villagers standing before them. Yup, five of them were down just from having passed through the palisade. Pretty good! Out of all the villagers, half of them were elderly. The ones who said they wouldn't mind dying to be a shield for their younger kin.

Roland and Emile appeared from one of the nearby houses to prevent that from happening. Though, really, they were just there to help any villagers who were in danger. Everyone else was on their own.

It went without saying for Francette, but Roland was also quite skilled, having received martial training ever since he was a child, so he was strong enough to fight off a few ordinary soldiers and knights. Bandits were no match. Especially because he had that divine sword, Exhovud. I had finally caved under his incessant complaining…

Oh, but it didn't come with any supersonic vibration functions. It was just durable, easy to maintain, and sharp. Roland was still really happy, though. How desperate to get a divine sword was he…?

I had told him the sword was top secret, and he wasn't to tell anyone about it.

By this point, the initial skirmish had ended. It was time for the main battle.

…I think I'll back up a bit.

"Mercenaries? But two or three more aren't gonna change anything! …Oh, I get it. You're the ones who put them up to this, aren't you? Screw this village, you're all gonna die! Then the next village we target will know to do as they're told! Watch your village burn, all due to your own stupid actions, and despair!"

The bandit leader was enraged from losing half of his men and seemed to abandon the idea of milking the villagers long-term. Now he had changed tactics to killing everyone here, then moving on to the next village to leech off of them. Not that these bandits could ever have leeched off of the very people who had killed nearly half of their men with indirect attacks. They would've had to worry about getting knifed in their sleep every night.

Once the villagers realized that the bandits could be easily killed, there was no way they'd ever put up with their unreasonable demands again. Especially considering that they had reduced their enemy numbers by half in the initial skirmish, all while taking zero casualties of their own...

And the sound of swords clashing rang in the air! Actually, one side didn't have swords, so I guess not. The bandits had their swords raised with the fences at their backs, while the villagers stood before them, stances low, with their spears pointed at their foes. The bandits' positioning was scattered and uncoordinated, while the villagers stayed close to each other, moving in on the bandits in a half-circle. A phalanx, I think it's called? Though they didn't have any shields.

Though it had a weakness to sudden flanking maneuvers and rear attacks, the phalanx was an impenetrable formation when there was no chance of hidden enemy reinforcements. Even if the bandits did have any forces in reserve, they would appear on the other side of the palisade, and there was no way for those reinforcements to take the villagers by surprise. Moreover, considering that it'd be an influx of untrained men wielding cheap, dull, poorly-maintained swords, there was no way they could have cleanly cut through the bamboo spears, even the ones that weren't secured firmly in the ground.

By the time the bandits realized that they were the hunted rather than the hunters, it was already too late. Trapped in this confined space, with the palisade at their backs, they couldn't get through the concentrated wall of spears thrust toward them, and thus found themselves helpless.

"Bastaaards!"

One of the bandits knocked a bamboo spear upward with his sword and tried to attack, but was promptly impaled with additional spears from both sides. Another bandit tried to slip through the bamboo spears, but then another villager appeared from behind two of the other spearmen and swung a three-pronged hoe down, straight into the man's skull.

There were plenty of men wielding farming tools right behind the spearmen, prepared to bring their tools down on any bandits who might approach. Those tools had more reach than the bandits' swords, and swords had the disadvantage of being ineffective with the arm fully extended. They had to get closer to get a proper swing in. On the other hand, garden hoes could be brought down upon their target with the arms fully outstretched.

Several of the panicking bandits turned to go back out through the palisade, but more villagers had moved around them with their bamboo spears at the ready. Some of those spear-wielding villagers included women and children, but they only needed to point their weapons at the bandits to fend them off. As for the bandits, they were trying to get through the narrow space between two palisade sections, with no room to swing their swords.

…They were done for.

But it seemed the bandit leader couldn't stand the thought of the infamous Beasts of Disaster, nearly thirty men in all, being taken down by mere villagers without even killing a single one of their opponents. He screamed in rage and tried to rush through the bamboo spears surrounding him. The villagers recognized that this was the decisive moment and all thrust their bamboo spears into the leader at once, then brought down their farming tools upon his body. After letting out a resentful growl, he finally sank to the ground.

Several other bandits followed, then the remaining men threw down their weapons and surrendered. The death penalty was pretty common around these parts, and captured bandits tended to become slaves for life rather than being executed, unless they were the type to ruthlessly murder entire caravans that had already surrendered to them. Being put to work in the mines as a slave was a harsh life, and one that often didn't last very long, but it was better than being killed on the spot. If they didn't cause any problems, there was a chance they could get moved to an easier, safer work environment for a healthier, longer life.

These bandits were apparently a wicked bunch, but the leader, second, and advisor had already been killed. So, even if we captured the remaining small fry instead of killing them, it was unlikely that they'd survive by themselves.

We rounded up the bandits who had surrendered, and the villagers stood around dazedly for some time. But they eventually came back to reality again, and raised their voices, giving cheers of jubilation.

Amidst the tumult of laughter and tears, I had Francette and Emile help me with a certain task. We were going around administering healing potions to the fallen bandits. If they were physically unable to drink, or refused to because they suspected it was poison, we poured the potion onto their wounds. Now that we had won, there was no need to let anyone else die.

It wasn't that I was being generous. I would turn them in to the city guards and have them receive the appropriate punishment for their crimes. If they were wanted "dead or alive," now that I had them captured, I would naturally just turn them in alive. There was no need to kill them first. Besides, if they died, it would be a pain to deal with all the rotting corpses and maggots.

But I was more concerned about the villagers killing their already-surrendered enemies once, and then doing so again in the future. With how things had unfolded until now, and the abuse they'd received from bandits in the past, it was possible that the villagers would have taken such action.

It would have been disturbing if the villagers ended up becoming a band of merciless killers, or went around murdering bandits in the name of justice. I didn't hold back if it was for self-defense, but I also didn't agree with deliberately going out to shed blood. We had to show them the importance of control and moderation.

There was also the most important reason of all...

If we turned the bandits in alive, we would not only get a monetary reward, but we would also get half of their worth when they're sold off as slaves!

...What's that? I just ruined everything I said?

...Anyway, we were tying up the living bandits, and pouring healing potions on the dying, when a young villager came running up in a hurry.

"If you're finishing them off, please let me do it!"

See?!

*   *

"...That's why there's no need to hold back in battle, but if you capture them alive, make sure to turn them in to the authorities! Otherwise, everyone will know that you'll kill even those who surrender, and no one will ever have reason to yield. That will only lead to more people needlessly dying and getting injured. You'll miss out on your cut of the criminals being sold as slaves, too..."

It seemed they understood where I was coming from, once I had given them an explanation. It wasn't that they had turned into a bloodthirsty mob, but they were just on a temporary high from all the adrenaline. Whew...

There were very few bandits whom we had captured alive, at least besides the ones who had surrendered in the end. If they had been smacked hard through their armor with dull swords, they may have gotten away with just fatal wounds like ruptured organs and broken bones.

...As in, they may have eventually been fatal, but they wouldn't have died instantly. But having been stabbed with multiple bamboo spears, most of them seemed to have died within a minute of sustaining their injuries. It wasn't as if bandits would ever wear plate armor...

Well, I guess there's not much you could do about that.

"Thank you so much! I will remember this for the rest of my life!"

Yeah, I don't think the rest of that old mayor's life is going to be very long...

Francette, Roland, and Emile had been watching the fight nervously, with their hands on their sword hilts, ready to help the villagers if they were in danger, but they ended up not having to step in.

We had planned on letting the villagers handle it themselves in the first place, so they had assumed they wouldn't need to get involved, and if they had needed to step in, it would've been if the villagers were completely incapable of doing it without help. In that case, we would have had Francette deal with the bandits, then told the villagers that they were on their own next time. But the villagers and the elderly had done it themselves.

223

Next time... If there was a next time, could they fend for themselves without me, the emergency backup, or the convenient Tekkon? And did they really have the guts to do it without any outside help? If they failed, it would be on us for egging them on...

No, forget that!

They had asked for help this time, so we helped. Nothing more, nothing less.

I can't take responsibility for everything that happens after. The rest is all up to them!

I'd just watch over them from afar. ...And not get involved. I couldn't protect every farming village, mountain village, and fishing village in the world!

The villagers had begun preparing for a feast. I decided to eat my fill, then take my leave. The food in this village, like that simmered stuff that looked like the tips of thick-stemmed bamboo, and that cloud ear mushroom-looking thing, was actually pretty good...

Francette didn't get to do much this time, but she wasn't in a bad mood or anything. She understood that it wouldn't have been a good thing if she had actually needed to step in. Emile, too, of course. As for Roland... it went without saying.

Now, time to go retrieve Layette and Belle...

*　　　*

"First, please send a messenger to the city. Have them take the bandits into custody, and get your reward payment and half of the proceeds for the sale of the criminals as slaves.

"...Don't do anything reckless like taking them into the city yourselves. Those bandits are crafty, so they'll complain about their bound hands hurting, or that they need to go relieve themselves, or they'll have sprained their ankles, and then try to kill their escorts to get away.

"Even if they're unarmed, they can easily kill someone who's not a trained fighter by snapping their neck, shoving a finger in their eye, or crushing their throat."

"..."

The villagers were looking a bit pale.

Ah...

Yeah, they were taking this too lightly.

"Make sure you have a specialist handle the escorting. Instead of hiring a hunter, you can ask the police to take in the bandits for free. And make sure you send three or four reliable people with them, so no one gets any funny ideas about the reward money and the commission. Even police officers might be tempted to make a little extra cash."

"..."

Are they shocked because I suspect the police?

Half of the commission for the sale of criminals as slaves went to the city, and the police officer who took them in got a cut... I mean, a bonus... so I was sure they'd be happy to bring in the captured bandits, but they were the kind of people who had ignored the village while it was in danger, so I didn't consider the police all that trustworthy.

Though, I suppose it's possible that it's a policy set by their superiors and it's not necessarily the fault of the individual officers...

Anyway, the food was being brought out, so it was time to eat and hightail it out of here! We were just outsiders, after all. We didn't belong in this village. To these people, we weren't all that different from the bandits: temporary irregularities. The village had been protected by the villagers themselves, not by some god that happened to pass by or a Deus Ex Machina that had wiped out the bandits for them.

I decided the meal and usage of their hot springs was payment enough to cover my consulting fee. It's like they say, *"I'll let you off easy this time!"*

...Well, I guess it's not really like that.

"Thank you, Miss Francette!"

It was the boy who had first brought us to the village. I looked over to find the hoe he was still gripping in his hand had some black-red blood caked onto it. ...Already battle-tested, eh?

This boy seemed to think Francette exercised the most authority in our group. Well, Roland and Francette were obviously the most important-looking just based on their equipment, and Roland tended to hold women in high esteem, particularly me and Francette, so it couldn't be helped if Francette looked to be at the top of the food chain... I mean, the hierarchy. And above all, Francette was the one who had put effort into training the boy in the use of the sword, and she was obviously more skilled than Roland, so the boy thought of Francette as the biggest authority figure among us.

"I'll train hard and buy a real sword instead of using farming tools! Then I'm gonna kill every bandit out there!"

He seemed to think Francette would praise and encourage him for killing the bandits, and for steeling his resolve to protect the village.

But Francette shook her head.

"Then you would no longer be a farmer."

"Huh...?"

He didn't understand what she was saying. The boy looked at Francette with a blank expression, and she continued:

"You mustn't learn martial arts just for the sake of killing other people. It must be to better yourself, and to protect those you care about. ...You may end up killing others, at times, as a result. But if you learn the martial arts because you wish to kill, that would make you more like a bandit than a knight or a farmer. Sir Roland and I did not teach you how to wield a sword for something like that.

"The people here fought bravely and drove off the bandits this time around, despite having no combat training. This victory wasn't achieved from a desire to kill the bandits, but everyone's genuine, desperate will and desire to protect their fellow villagers. Protecting the village is not about an eager drive to murder...

"It's about everyone in the village cooperating together, and having a strong will. You certainly don't need a bloodthirsty killer among you to accomplish that."

He clearly didn't understand everything Francette had said, but the boy did seem to get the gist of it. His right hand holding the hoe loosened its grip, and he nodded. The adults around Francette who had been listening would likely repeat what she had said to the children later.

The young adults, who had been getting overly excited and rowdy, quieted down, and the mood grew heavy. But the old men used the wisdom of their years and raised their voices to liven up the feast once more. They produced what seemed to be their secret stash of mead and alcohol, made from local fruits and grains, but since the captured bandits were still around, my group and a portion of the villagers held back on any alcohol intake.

We chose to eat the best dishes offered, said our farewells to the mayor and a few of the older villagers, then slipped out of the feast, which would likely go on for some time. The elderly villagers sensed that we didn't want to stay long, so they gave us their thanks and saw us off. Being rich with experience, it seemed they were rather perceptive about this sort of thing.

Oh, and I advised them to disarm all those traps we had prepared but ended up not using. I didn't want the villagers to accidentally get caught in one of them, after all. They may have gone unused this time, but setting those traps was a useful experience, so it definitely wasn't a waste. Failures and mistakes are useful, so long as they contribute to the next attempt. Nothing in life is a waste. All those times I had to clash with my shitty superiors and supervisors helped me level up my patience and ability to ignore irritating things, so they weren't wasted.

Yeah, I'm sure of it!

* *

Francette seemed to be deep in thought as we walked down a mountain path that was little more than an animal trail.

"Is something bothering you?"

"Oh, no... I was just thinking about that village..."

I tried talking to her, but it seemed she wasn't too deep in thought. It was just on her mind a bit.

"A small village manages to survive by enduring exploitation from bandits, and without handing over their food and their girls, but now that they've learned to fight back, you're worried about whether they can keep it up. Is that it?"

"...Yes. Once they start fighting back, one mistake will lead to the destruction of the entire village. And there's no guarantee that it will always go well like it did this time..."

That much was obvious. Fortune decides the outcome of any given battle.

"They may all get wiped out someday."

"Y-You say that so dryly…"

Francette's eyes widened, but it was the truth.

"Depending on the scale they're dealing with, it's up to the villagers to decide to fight or do as they're told like before. It's not as if they always have to fight. And no matter what they choose and how things end up, they now have the freedom of choice. All we did was give them a free trial run with a safety net this one time, and one extra option moving forward. Whatever they do now isn't our concern, and we can't be responsible for it. That's all there is to it."

"…"

Francette was rather hardheaded and obsessed with justice.

Even though she's around thirty… Whoa!!!

Yeah, I had just narrowly avoided a boomerang thrown at me. That would've been fatal…

Anyway, it was all over with. There was nothing we could do now. So, we were going to spend some time at the hot spring and depart after enjoying another soak in the morning.

After all, the goal of this entire trip was to go on a staff vacation and visit hot springs. It was an episode of "Witnessed by the Housekeeper! College Girls Hot Spring Gourmet Timetable Murder Case!" Yes, the hot spring was all that mattered! Everything else was the whims of the Goddess.

I had just so happened to come across someone and decided to help them through their trouble. It was a singular, fortunate event. It absolutely didn't mean I would take care of them forever. That's just how it was.

We arrived at the hot springs, so I shooed Roland and Emile away and immediately got into the water.

What's that? The women got to go in first last time too? Women take longer, so maybe the guys should go in first, you say? I don't care! Hmm, Francette seems to be deep in thought. I think I'll modify the lion head to increase its healing effects and add a relaxation effect, too. And... there.

Hm? Wait a minute. I feel like I'm forgetting something... Oh!

"Belle, Francette, can you come over here?"

And as the girls and I enjoyed the hot spring together...

"Who goes there?!" Francette called out in a low, sharp voice. She immediately picked up her sword, which lay next to a nearby rock, taking a fighting stance with her sword's point toward the shadows.

Belle and I positioned ourselves to protect Layette and backed up a bit, with our bodies still in the water.

Then...

"What happened?!"

"Lady Kaoru!!!"

Roland and Emile popped out of the bushes behind us, swords drawn. Then they froze, standing bolt upright, their faces tight...

There was nothing and no one in the direction Francette was pointing her sword.

Francette's face turned toward Roland and Emile.

Likewise, Belle, Layette, and I also turned toward the two men.

Roland and Emile turned pale in response.

Our faces distorted in anger, and our bodies were neatly covered with towels.

"I wonder...where have you two been, and what were you doing? Why did you think there was trouble when Francette spoke in such a low voice? When the villager kids appeared the first time, how did you show up so quickly? I wonder... I wonder... I wonder...?"

"Gya..."

"Gya?"

"Gyaaaaaaaaagh!!!"

And so, the trial had begun.

"Guilty!"

"Guiltyyy!"

"Already?! That was a quick decision!!!"

It was time for Roland and Emile to receive their punishment. If I had let Francette punish Roland and Belle punish Emile, they would have gone easy on them, so I made them swap. Then, I whispered in their ears.

"Belle. Roland tried to peep on you and I while we were naked."

Tching!

Belle's face contorted with rage. Then...

"Francette. Emile tried to peep on you and I while we were naked."

Fwsh...

All the emotion drained from Francette's face.

Roland and Emile turned chalk-white.

"W-Wait..."

"H-Help..."

Not my problem!

In fact...

"Did you two think I wasn't mad, too?"

"But we aren't interested in you and Layette..."

Snap!

"Gyaaaaaa!!!"

...I messed up. I had turned up the hot spring's healing effects for Francette, so when Roland and Emile went in later, they recovered right away.

Damn...

The next day, we had another leisurely soak in the hot spring and made our way home, full of energy...

Completely forgetting that I had set the lion head to increase the water's healing properties and relaxation effects, without ever removing it...

Extra Story:
Roland's Melancholy

What can I do…?

One day, Francette had suddenly come to the royal palace and said that she would follow Kaoru, and that she wanted to cancel our engagement. Surprised, I had asked her what it was about, and she had informed me of the earth-shaking news that Kaoru was departing from the kingdom! Actually, that she wanted to cancel our engagement was an even greater incident! I had asked her for details in a panic, and I found out that Kaoru's reason for her journey was to find herself a partner! If that happened, Kaoru would stay wherever she found her partner, and our kingdom would lose the protection of the Goddess.

Not only that, but there were sure to be rumors about our kingdom driving away the Goddess, or that we had been abandoned by the Goddess, and those would quickly get out of hand.

Plus, Francette would likely follow Kaoru and stay wherever she ended up! That's just how she was! This meant our nation would not only lose our Goddess, but we would lose Francette, who was known as our 'great hero,' the 'guardian of the kingdom,' and, of course, 'Fearsome Fran.'

…And I would lose my fiancee. I, a man of the royal family, would be one-sidedly abandoned by my betrothed.

Gyaaaaaaaaa!!! I-I can't let that happen! I-I must prevent that, no matter what!

But I couldn't use my station or physical force to stop Kaoru.

Wh-What should I do…?

I know!!!

"I will go with you!"

"Huh…?" Francette looked at me, wide-eyed, but I didn't care!

There's no escape! I won't let you or Kaoru get away, Francette!!!

…And so, here we are.

As Kaoru's companion, Francette and I were on an eventful journey with two kids and a younger child.

Emile is sixteen, so he's not a kid anymore? Sixteen is still a little brat! Definitely a kid!

Francette was now sleeping next to me.

…In the bed next to mine! She said we wouldn't share a bed until we were married, but I knew what she was really thinking. If she got pregnant, she wouldn't be able to continue traveling with Kaoru.

I mean, unlike commoners, nobles and royals sought purity and celibacy from their marriage partners, so she wasn't wrong to hold out until marriage. Bloodline was everything to nobles and royals.

But we were engaged, so how about a little, you know…

Damn it!

Then when would Kaoru's journey end so we could return to the kingdom and get married? And if Kaoru decided to live somewhere else, would Francette come back to the kingdom? And would Kaoru, who didn't look any different after all these years and could have been tens of thousands of years old but still hadn't found a marriage partner, be able to find someone to marry in the next ten or twenty years? Would her marriage partner even be human? If she was looking for a god roaming the human realm like herself, maybe it was going to take hundreds, if not thousands, of years.

…Francette and I wouldn't be alive that long! Wait, I'd known Francette for over four years now, but it didn't seem like she'd aged since… No no no, I was concerned about that before and asked Kaoru about it behind Francette's back once.

She told me, "I don't think I added an anti-aging effect to that potion…"

That's what she said, anyway. Her questionable phrasing made me a bit anxious, but I chose to believe it didn't have any such effects…

Anyway, this was a troubling situation. Pretty bad, in fact.

The way Kaoru was looking to other countries for procreation, how Francette always followed Kaoru around, the way I always got brushed aside, everything! All I could do was sabotage things from behind the scenes to prevent Kaoru from hooking up with someone from another country, but Francette stuck her head out from the alley to watch over Kaoru's shop every day. From morning to night… No, even through the night…

Francette seemed to have limitless energy, but I felt like she was looking a little tired as of late… Wait, when did she sleep, anyway? Oh no. Come to think of it, the situation may have been worse than I imagined.

If Francette fell ill… well, I guess we had Kaoru's potions. If Francette made a mistake due to fatigue and lack of sleep, getting injured as a result… well, I guess we had Kaoru's potions. I mean, even if she did slip up from being so tired, she'd probably get away with a minor scrape. It was hard to imagine Fearsome Fran would sustain an injury from an enemy force of less than a thousand men.

Those who aren't from our kingdom seem to think that that's some story we made up to make her seem like a hero, but Francette would actually pull it off. She'd take on one or two thousand with relative ease...

She hadn't gotten her nickname for nothing.

Anyway, this was bad! No matter what anyone said, this was a dire situation! Francette and I had been training Emile to get stronger, but he had a long way to go. He could probably take on five or six common thugs at once. If we were dealing with trained soldiers, or Rank C hunters or higher, maybe two or three opponents at once would be the best he could hope for.

Belle? She may have managed to take out one person in exchange for her own life, or stop a knife by being a human shield, but that would be it. Kaoru would never let that happen, though. Realistically, all Belle could do was watch over Layette.

Anyway, there's no need for Francette to be so worried about Kaoru in the first place. Francette has seen what Kaoru is capable of, many times, with her own eyes. Those who have tried to harm Kaoru have had their heads blown up, have dropped to the floor spitting out blood, and been struck with lightning. We've even seen her run through the chest with a blade and still be fine...

I tried to convince Francette not to be so extreme with her attempts to protect Kaoru, primarily by arguing that Kaoru would be saddened if something happened to her from overworking herself, but she responded, *"What if something unexpected happened to her?!"* and *"What if Lady Kaoru abandoned humankind because we upset her, and she ascended to heaven?!"*, firming up her resolve even further...

Ahhh, what was I supposed to do...?

It had been problem after problem, lately, and the only good thing that had happened recently was Kaoru gifting me a sword...

I had been trying to convince her to do that every single day, and she finally granted me the divine sword Exhovud upon declaring, *"Aaagh! Shaddap! Fine! Just leave me alone already!"*

It may have been inferior to Francette's Exgram, but was comparable to the swords bestowed to the four royal guards, the Exhrotti. Unbreaking, unbending, easy to maintain because it repelled blood, and it never lost its sharpness. Truly a weapon made for the lazy. Its ease of maintenance was one thing, but the fact that it never broke despite how rough it was treated gave it a great sense of reliability.

Kaoru had indicated many times that the fact that a member of the royal line had received a divine sword must be kept a complete secret, but that much was obvious. Even an idiot would know it would be bad if word got out that a member of the royal family had received a divine sword from a goddess. Some would scheme to take advantage of it, and the religious factions like the Temple of the Goddess would start making political moves, and most of all, my brother Serge's claim to the throne would be in danger.

It was very unfortunate that I couldn't brag about my sword, but this was one secret I had to keep. The fact that I had a divine sword still remained, so I had no reason to complain.

A divine sword...

The weapon I had always wanted, granted only to heroes chosen by divinity!

Ahh! Ahhh! Aaaaaahhh!!! Haah... Haah... Whew, I got a little excited...

*   *

Soon, we were going to arrive at Beliscas, the town where we planned on staying next.

"Kaoru, I wanted to ask you for a favor…"

Hm? Francette's asking Kaoru for something.

"What is it?"

"I want to be someone who can live with you in your next 'backstory.' It's a bit too difficult to keep watch over you at all times when we live in separate residences…"

"Of course it would be difficult! What did… Wait, why were you watching me at all times in the first place?!"

Was she crazy?! I couldn't believe she was planning on watching over Kaoru all day while living separately. Anyone other than Francette would have fallen unconscious from fatigue by now.

But now, Kaoru would likely accommodate Francette's request in her backstory. It would all be fine now… Wait. Wait a second! What did Francette just say?

"I want to be someone who can live with you…"

"I want to be someone who…"

"I want to…"

"I…" "I…" "I…"

Why "I" and not "we"? What about me? What about meeeeee!!!

Afterword

This is FUNA.

Thank you so much for reading volume four of *I Shall Survive Using Potions!* Season one of *Potions* ended with the publication of volume two. The series was originally expected to end in one season, but we shattered those plans with season two going strong! And the overseas version is ongoing too! This is all thanks to all you readers. Thank you again! Kaoru and company have arrived in a new city.

This time, she will start a normal life... or so she thinks.

But trouble just seems to always come find her.

Geezers, horses... and bandits! And in volume five, some annoying people to deal with...

Kaoru: "Here we go!" Francette: "Ah... They've made Kaoru mad..." Volume three of the comic version is out along with this book, and volume four of the light novel and volume three of the comics for *Saving 80,000 Gold in Another World for my Retirement* are also out now! The FUNA festival is going strong! The ongoing comic version is updated every first and third Monday on the webcomic magazine, "Suiyoubi no Sirius"! (http://seiga.nicovideo. jp/manga/official/w_sirius/) If you forget it's updated on Mondays and don't keep up with the series... In the name of the Mo(o)n(day), I'll punish you! As long as this series is still ongoing, I get to go to the annual Kodansha Ranobe Bunko anniversary party and eat free food! (Ranobe Bunko and K Ranobe Books have the same editing department.)

And along with *Potions*, I will use the anime adaptation of *Didn't I Say to Make My Abilities Average in the Next Life?!* to increase my sales even further! And so, I've moved another step closer to my ambitions...

To my editor; the illustrator, Sukima; the binding designer, the proofreader, and others; the printer, distributor, and bookstores; the light novel submission website, Shōsetsuka ni Narō; everyone who pointed out errors or provided advice in the feedback section; and everyone who picked up this book, I appreciate you all from the bottom of my heart.

Thank you! I hope to see you again in the next volume...

FUNA